THE ACHIEVERS

THE ACHIEVERS

Raymond C. Johnson

The Art of Self-Management for Success

* *

T·T

TRUMAN TALLEY BOOKS
E. P. DUTTON
NEW YORK

The quotation on pages 176–77 is from the *Dear Padre Bulletin* (September 8, 1985), written by Father Joe Morin, CSSR. Reprinted by permission of Liguori Publications, Liguori, Missouri.

This publication is designed to provide accurate and authoritative information in regard to the subject matter covered. It is sold with the understanding that the publisher is not engaged in rendering legal, accounting, or other professional service. If legal advice or other expert assistance is required, the service of a competent professional person should be sought.

Published in the United States by
Truman Talley Books • E. P. Dutton,
a division of New American Library,
2 Park Avenue, New York, N.Y. 10016.

Library of Congress Cataloging-in-Publication Data
Johnson, Raymond (Raymond C.)
The achievers.
"A Truman Talley book."
Includes index.
1. Success in business. 2. Achievement motivation.
I. Title.
HF5386.J63   1987   650.1   86-13556
ISBN 0-525-24396-8

Published simultaneously in Canada by
Fitzhenry & Whiteside Limited, Toronto

DESIGNED BY EARL TIDWELL

10 9 8 7 6 5 4 3 2 1

First Edition

To my wife, Alice,
in appreciation
for her help and encouragement

CONTENTS

WHY THIS BOOK

Had I but known in my early years what I now know, how much more I could have accomplished in my lifetime—with so much less sweat and tears.
—THE AUTHOR

This book was motivated by the recognition that today is the day of the achiever. Never in our history have achievers received so much recognition and public acclamation. This recognition and acclamation is by far the greatest attitude change that business has undergone over these past twenty years.

Our excellent graduate schools of business are turning out more graduates than ever before. These young people are receiving starting salaries ranging between

$35,000 and $40,000 a year—unthinkable a decade ago. What a time this is to be an achiever!

However, a formal education, no matter how fine, is essentially only a door opener. The individual who aspires to the summit must have additional resources. To know from classroom study the "science of management" is important, but *more important* is mastering the "art of self-management." Much has been written about science versus art. Fowler, in his *Dictionary of Modern English Usage*, points out the differences: "Science knows, Art does; Science is a body of connected facts, Art is a set of directions; the facts of science are the same for all people, circumstances and occasions; the directions of art vary with the artist and the task."

The distinction as commonly understood is that science is concerned with theoretical truth and art with the methods of ascertaining certain results.

This book is devoted to the *art* of attaining certain results and of becoming an achiever. It has little to do with management but it examines the manager, the leader, and how he or she became one. It will show you how you can belong to this distinguished group in your chosen field of endeavor.

Achievers are a heterogeneous group from all walks of life and from many different backgrounds. Because achievement is not the result of any *one* method or technique, achievers in addition to their formal education have to develop skills. Skills, techniques, and personality traits are rarely emphasized in classroom textbooks and are *not* often taught in schools, colleges, or graduate schools. There is no pill one can swallow to become an achiever immediately. The techniques that make achievers are learned and developed through years of experience, in what used to be called "the College of Hard Knocks." Sometimes the lessons were learned too late.

This book will help you acquire the invaluable techniques and skills now. It will enable you to bypass trial and error and the frustration of long experience. It will assume that you are well versed in the science or theoretical truth pertinent to your work. It will stress the need for self-management: the art of attaining certain beneficial results that will enable you to expand the perimeters of your classroom skills. It will document and analyze in depth the techniques, the on-the-job methods of acknowledged achievers, to help you make the most of your own talents.

The author concentrates on practical matters through the use of true stories. You will see how techniques and personality traits relate to and feed on each other. Sometimes that relationship is positive and sometimes negative. They are, in a word, *synergistic.* An understanding of them is vital in the keen competition of today's marketplace. You can make that synergism work for you. It is not any one thing you do, but the total effect of *all* the things you do, both bad and good, that makes or breaks your personal quest for ultimate success.

What a time to be an achiever—on the baseball diamond or the football field; in the media, the films, the stage, the literary world; in serious music or rock; in the operating room or in the courtroom; in executive suites of corporations or in Wall Street brokerage offices. The aspiring achiever sees all those around him or her who have made it—not by luck but by mastering the required skills and techniques. The truly knowledgeable have taken over the marketplace. For the first time the achiever in almost every walk of life is being recognized and compensated for the profits he or she generates for an organization without regard to age, seniority, or past experience.

The prime purpose of this book is to help you become the man or the woman who will achieve your objectives in life and will experience the joy of overcoming all obstacles and succeed in what you start out to do.

THE ACHIEVERS

1

ELEVATE YOUR SIGHTS

A career, like a business, must be budgeted. When it is necessary, the budget can be adjusted to meet changing conditions. A life that hasn't a definite plan is likely to become driftwood.
—DAVID SARNOFF

Putting first things first, it is vitally important that you carefully reexamine your ultimate goal. Just where are you heading in this career—this *life* of yours? *Don't sell yourself short!* Despite popular belief to the contrary, there is not an enormous difference in ability between the achievers and the nonachievers. As an example, it does not follow that the salesman who earns $200,000 a year must have ten times as much ability as a $20,000-a-year salesman who covers the same territory with the same line.

A willingness to accept such illogical thinking can steer you into a niche where you become someone who barely manages to get by instead of realizing your potential to become an achiever who gets to the top. This kind of negative and discouraging thinking can actually prevent you from trying to improve your lot; it can make you lose hope to the point that you feel it's futile even to make the effort.

Measuring the Gap Between the Winner and the Also-Ran

The gap between the winner and the also-ran is often very small. Closing that real or imagined gap is a very worthwhile achievement in itself. To illustrate the often-tiny margin between greatness and mediocrity, let's look at the field of sports, where the difference between contenders and champions can actually be measured.

One of the great horse races of all time took place one Saturday afternoon at a racetrack near Arcadia, California. A record crowd of more than seventy-five thousand packed the grandstand and the rails for the running of the $100,000 Santa Anita Handicap. Few of the spectators really expected a close race; most had made the trip for a chance to see the odds-on favorite, the mighty Seabiscuit, strut his stuff. Hardly anyone expected a serious challenge from a little-known horse called Whichcee, rated by most handicappers as a rank outsider. But it quickly became evident that Whichcee had other ideas. He broke furiously from the starting gate to set the pace, clung to the number one position at the quarter-mile pole, and continued to lead at the three-quarters mark.

As the horses entered the stretch, the great Seabiscuit, purposely biding his time, steadily began to move up and eventually nosed ahead. But the gallant Whichcee refused to quit. The lead seesawed back and forth in the closing yards, forcing the spectators to their feet in a frenzy of excitement. With a final burst of speed, Seabiscuit lunged ahead and crossed the wire as the winner, breaking the track record and becoming—at the time—the greatest money-winner ever.

Seabiscuit, of course, has become a fabled name, arguably one of the greatest Thoroughbreds in the history of racing. But what about Whichcee, the determined horse that was pounding at the famous one's heels a scant two lengths behind at the wire? That horse was soon forgotten, even by those who saw the race. Yet the difference between the legendary winner and the also-ran was only a few yards.

Why talk about horses? Good point! Let's talk about people and the difference between the leaders and the average man and woman. That difference is even better illustrated in major-league baseball. Statistics reveal that, on average, a big-league player compiles a career batting average close to the .250 mark. In other words, most players will average one base hit in every four trips to the plate during their playing days. Most of us are familiar with the names of notable exceptions to that norm—names like Cobb, Hornsby, DiMaggio, Williams, Musial, and Rose. Today we thrill at the emergence of new young hitting stars like Don Mattingly and Willie McGee, men who have demonstrated that they are capable of hitting the ball consistently at a .350 clip.

Although many journeymen big-league players must settle for the minimum major-league salary of $60,000 per season, the superstars can demand and receive a yearly stipend of well over $1 million a year. In light of that, it's interesting to take a closer look at the statistical differences between batting averages of .350 and .250. The disparity between greatness and mediocrity, on paper, amounts to a little more than one extra base hit every ten times at bat. Add the fact that most putouts at first are made with a margin of only a few inches, and it becomes clear that the measurable distinction between a journeyman and a superstar is small indeed.

Few of baseball's great heroes will hold to the belief that they were simply born with extraordinary talents that propelled them to the top. Most will admit that they were keen students of the game who systematically perfected their skills by making some slight improvement in batting stance, changing the grip on the bat, improving the takeoff from the batter's box or actual running stride to make up for those possible lost inches in the race for first. That extra thought and effort provided the additional base hits that enabled them to become .350 hitters and move into the big money.

Your Workplace Is Your Track or Batter's Box

These stories of accomplishment on the racetrack and the baseball diamond illustrate truths that are just as applicable in the competitive world of business as they are in the field of sports. Take time to reconsider both your goals and your potential. Is what you have to offer really so inferior? What separates you from those who are reaping the praise and rewards? Take heart—you can improve your performance!

Douglas Lurton is a man who has inspired thousands; as quoted in *The Forbes Scrapbook of Thoughts on the Business of Life* (New York: Forbes Publishing, 1976), he summed it up well: "It takes just a little more than the ordinary to move out ahead of the herd. Men and women do not achieve success by being *twice* as good as the other fellow. The very moment a man adds *just a little plus,* his results and his income increase in geometric proportions."

In sports, in the arts and professions, and in business, the margin between the winners and the also-rans is usually minuscule. To wipe out that small margin and achieve your personal goals, you only have to be *just a little bit better!*

THE BOTTOM LINE

1. The difference between ourselves and the achievers we should like to be is not at all insurmountable.

2. It's a small improvement in the way we go about our jobs that will bring a tremendous improvement in our results.

2

WORK:
A FOUR-LETTER
WORD?

I am glad that the eight-hour day had not been invented when I was a young man. If my life had been made up of eight-hour days I do not believe I could have accomplished a great deal.
—THOMAS A. EDISON

A favorite bromide of one of our great achievers is "I am a great believer in luck. The harder I work the luckier I get!" Achievers work to get the job done. They have learned that hard work takes the place of luck and can be counted on. The one characteristic all achievers have in common is they are workers.

A busy executive related an interesting discovery he made unexpectedly a few years ago. He flew into Cleveland to attend a conference. He took a taxi from the airport to the downtown area. Driving along Euclid

Avenue, he passed a large bookstore whose windows were filled with hundreds of copies of a single book titled *How to Avoid Work.* Intrigued, he stopped the cab, paid off the cabdriver, went into the store, and bought a copy. True to its labeling, the book turned out to be a most constructive and thorough examination of that unorthodox subject. However, the thrust of the treatise boiled down to one conclusion: love what you are doing and it ceases to be work; it becomes, instead, a joy and a pleasure.

Dr. John Schindler, as quoted in *Forbes Scrapbook,* sums it up in a very few words: "If a person likes to work and has learned the simple joy of doing something well, if he feels pleased at producing something of value to society, he will be generating pleasant emotions for himself at the time he is working, as well as for the man who hires him."

The "lucky" ones are privileged to work at something they enjoy. There is strong evidence that those who do find pleasure in their work are not only the happiest but also among the most successful people on earth. They are the hard workers who look forward to the morning when they can return to the challenges of their jobs.

If you find your work boring, frustrating, stultifying, completely lacking in challenge because it fails to make use of your best talents, then the sooner you change your job the better it will be for your career and for your chances of achieving your goals in life.

•

Job Stress and What It Can Teach Us

Blessed indeed is the individual who gains knowledge of his aptitudes and makes the right decision early in life on the goals he intends to pursue. Others, once committed, may find that their career choices were based on completely material considerations rather than long-term satisfaction.

Much has been written in recent years about "executive burnout," on the effects of stress in the workplace. Common sense tells us that some occupations are naturally more stressful than others. Self-analysis also reveals that we sometimes create unnecessary feelings of stress because of our own lack of preparation and confidence.

A professor at the University of Manchester's Institute of Science and Technology in England recently completed a scientific study of on-the-job pressures in fifty standard occupations. His staff of six researchers conducted extensive interviews with a large sampling of workers in the different occupations. Their findings, as reprinted in *Bits and Pieces*, a publication of the Economics Press in Fairfield, New Jersey, may just enable you to determine whether the amount of stress you feel is normal. The British researchers rated the stress factor for each occupation on a scale of 1 to 10, 10 being the most stressful.

The Manchester Study

Miner	8.3	Commercial pilot	7.5
Police officer	7.7	Prison officer	7.5
Construction worker	7.5	Advertising executive	7.3
Journalist	7.5	Dentist	7.3

Actor	7.2	Engineer	4.3
Politician	7.0	Real estate broker	4.3
Doctor	6.8	Hairdresser	4.3
Tax collector	6.8	Secretary	4.3
Film producer	6.5	Lawyer	4.3
Nurse	6.5	Artist, Designer	4.2
Fireman	6.3	Architect	4.0
Musician	6.3	Optician	4.0
Teacher	6.2	Local government	
Personnel director	6.0	planner	4.0
Social director	6.0	Mail carrier	4.0
Manager	5.8	Statistician	4.0
Public relations	5.8	Lab technician	3.8
Salesman	5.7	Banker	3.7
Stockbroker	5.5	Computer operator	3.7
Bus driver	5.4	Occupational	
Psychologist	5.2	therapist	3.7
Publishing executive	5.0	Linguist	3.7
Diplomat	4.8	Clergyman	3.5
Farmer	4.8	Astronomer	3.4
Soldier	4.7	Nursery-school	
Veterinarian	4.5	teacher	3.3
Government worker	4.4	Museum worker	2.8
Accountant	4.3	Librarian	2.0

The coal miner has the most stressful job, followed by the police officer and the construction worker. The librarian has the least stressful job, followed by the museum worker and the nursery-school teacher.

Your enthusiasm or your dislike for your job may be related to the amount of stress. Consider the possibility that you may in an unsuitable line of work. A stressful

occupation will not bother the person who likes challenge, excitement, even danger on the job. It motivates
those who enjoy working against time on a tight schedule. They like the pressure, but if you are a person who
wants peace and quiet, look for an occupation at the
lower end of the stress scale.

Learning the True Value of Work

There will probably always be clock-watchers who will
forever wonder why they failed to achieve the success
they are envious of others' having achieved. These people are usually well educated, but they never realize the
value of *work*: they do not realize that work pays off;
they never recognize opportunity when it knocks at
their door.

Here is the exciting story of John Fox, who certainly recognized a golden opportunity when it knocked. He
had a willingness to work hard and a determination to
forge ahead.

John Fox was born in England and raised in Atlantic City, New Jersey. Every summer as a boy he worked
as a bellhop in the Chelsea Hotel, and later he ran a salt-
water taffy machine at a boardwalk stand.

John was a worker and he made up his mind that he
would get a college education.

He achieved his goal by working at several jobs. He
ran a gas station, he sold shoes on campus, and he waited
on tables for four years—all helping to pay for part of
his tuition. John was graduated from Colgate University,
and over the next five years he paid off the balance

of his tuition. There were no student loans in his day to help him. He had to work his way through unassisted.

He continued to work hard through the years and became a vice-president of the National Research Corportion. It was here that the concept for concentrating orange juice by means of low temperature was developed.

John says:

No one approached me with the idea. I *asked* for the *opportunity* to form a company to exploit the concept, and the board of directors gave me the green light.

I did not raise the initial capital from friends and relatives but with a public offering for $2,650,000.

The first plant we built was designed to produce a freeze-dried orange juice powder destined for the military hospitals. This part of the plant never worked properly, so we abandoned the powder product and went to market with the first frozen orange juice concentrate, which we made in preliminary phase to the powder dryers.

At this juncture I did run out of funds, but my rescue came from Jock Whitney and his venture-capital firm. It was Jock who introduced me to Bing [Crosby], who agreed to put on a 15-minute radio show one day a week in exchange for 20,000 shares of our then-worthless stock. Our real stroke of luck happened when Bing gave some of his stock to his scriptwriters. They wrote plugs for Minute Maid in nearly every public utterance Bing made.

Bing's national radio show not only succeeded in selling the public on the idea of a delicious new product but also brought in swarms of new investors. This badly needed new money gave Fox's engineers time to overcome the flaws in the manufacturing process and provide adequate working capital. Minute Maid quickly became one of the most successful new enterprises in America.

After his years of success as president of Minute Maid, Fox agreed to sell his interest in the company to Coca-Cola.

Later his reputation for diligence and hard work brought him the offer of the presidency of the United Fruit Company. He accepted and eventually became chairman of the board of this mammoth company.

It's a simple truth that men and women who finally achieve positions of leadership do so only after much thought and action and long periods of dedicated work. The rare individual who rises to the top because he has inherited his wealth (and possibly his position) stays there only as long as he is able to produce. With all the opportunities today provided by new industries that demand highly trained workers, there is a real danger that some who have recently entered the work force will relax, concentrate on their current success, and overlook the big picture. That's a natural but dangerous practice. Too many capable young people, eagerly recruited from the college campuses, run the risk of falling into the corporate rut—contributing just enough to get by. Only hard work and careful planning can keep that rut from getting deeper, propelling the unwary out the back door.

David Sarnoff, the founder and longtime chief executive of the Radio Corporation of America, had wise advice for people with that attitude, words that are as applicable today as they were the day he first uttered them:

"Don't be misled into thinking the world owes you a living. The boy who believes his parents, or the government, or anyone else owes him his livelihood and that he can collect it without labor will wake up one day and find himself working for another boy who did not have that belief and, therefore, earned the right to have others work for him."

Modern research has verified that "all work and no play" will make ol' Jack a *sick* as well as a dull boy. So-called workaholism can be destructive to both the personal health and the family life of a person who loses sight of the need to budget his time. The proper harnessing of intellectual and physical energy is another primary element in the "art of self-management" that must be learned by anyone striving for ultimate success. The choice becomes clearer with an exercise in word coinage. If a truly dedicated worker can be called a workaholic, doesn't it follow that the individual who won't give his best effort could be labeled a restaholic?

Thomas A. Edison, undeniably one of the greatest achievers in history, is reputed to have been so engrossed in his work that he slept ony three hours out of each twenty-four. The incandescent flame of his brilliance continues to glow in every light bulb in the world today, and he lived to a very active old age. We can't all expect to come equipped with either Edison's gifts or his stamina, but his example of dedication to his work has been echoed time and again by those who have been determined to do more than merely "put in their time."

Industrialist Andrew Carnegie, for example, said: "The average person puts only 25 percent of his energy and ability into his work. The world takes off its hat to those who put in more than 50 percent of their capacity, and stands on its head for those few and far between souls who devote 100 percent."

The road to the top, in almost any job or profession, is more open today than it has ever been. Your first step on that road must be an intelligent and persistent attention to your work.

THE BOTTOM LINE

1. Establish a clear definition of the word *work*. The average person knows what it means to his bank account. The achiever appreciates what it means to his *life*.

2. The mediocre put in their time for the company. The exceptional make the company's time work for *them*.

3

FIND THE RIGHT WORK

I do not despise genius—indeed, I wish I had a basketful of it. But yet, after a great deal of experience and observation, I have become convinced that industry is a better horse to ride than genius. It may never carry any man as far as genius has carried individuals, but industry—patient, steady, intelligent industry—will carry thousands into comfort, and even celebrity; and this it does with absolute certainty.

—WALTER LIPPMANN

One of the greatest strengths of the United States is the opportunity for any industrious, motivated individuals to prosper and strive toward their highest goals. Today, new figures reveal that some seventeen out of every ten thousand Americans have actually become millionaires. That is a mind-boggling statistic. Even more astounding is the fact that a full quarter of these people are still under the age of fifty.

While this sizable percentage of our population is achieving this impressive economic status and its resulting public acclaim, many others just drift away from their hopes and dreams that were so much a part of their lives when they left their institutions of higher learning. They leap at jobs that offer enticing salaries; all too often that decision marks the beginning of the end of their aspirations to become real achievers.

Common sense tells us that we must accept the reality that there can't be more generals than private soldiers. On the other hand, there is also truth in the premise of author-columnist Walter Lippmann that industry can be, for the majority of us, as valuable as genius. There is little doubt that those who have succeeded in boosting themselves into positions of great wealth, prestige, and power have reveled in the planning, the ups-and-downs—all the struggle that it took to get them to the place they had planned to go. Quite simply, the ultimate achievement of the individual who stands out from the crowd is a direct reflection of the exhilaration and happiness he found in his work.

But what of the educated, seemingly capable person who is unable to rise at a pace in keeping with his intelligence and training? The obvious answer would be that he or she is either basically lazy or totally ignorant of the vital self-management skills that we shall be discussing in the chapters of this book. However, as any good manager would with an employee who is at least *adequate*, let's give this individual the benefit of the doubt and examine his situation more closely.

Does he put in his hours and perform his duties well but evince little enthusiasm or initiative? On the other hand, does he regale his fellow workers with the excitement of his latest round of golf or drama on the tennis court? Is he the office expert on the newest escapist film or novel, but the first member of the staff to beg off when told about an interesting new training course connected with his job? Does he "come to life" and assume a more vital personality immediately after he waves his farewell to the office receptionist?

A person like this is obviously bored with his job, the place where he spends half of his waking hours. He is equipped to handle it but misses a challenge and pours his abilities and enthusiasm into outside interests. The tragedy is that he is unknowingly shortchanging himself as well as his employer. Both would be better served if the employee would begin thinking about finding the right work—work in which he must utilize all the imagination and vigor that he dissipates on pursuits that deflate rather than increase his income.

The Right Work—*Fulfillment of a Fantasy?*

There are few Gauguins among us who are adventurous enough to cast aside a successful business career and sail to Tahiti to start anew as a painter. To suggest that a well-paid corporate lawyer leave his firm and start over in the medical profession because he was so spiritually uplifted by an episode of "St. Elsewhere" is ridiculous. On the other hand, an individual who is bogged down in work that is uninspiring has every reason to begin a careful exploration of opportunities in another area where he can put his experience and ability to better use. Oftentimes, the work in which he will find both pleasure and success is not too far afield from the job that is carrying him to a dead end.

Our history is filled with stories of men and women

who found satisfaction and success by striking out in new directions. One such true incident involved a man we'll call James Sloan. As a child Jimmie's first love was for anything and everything of a mechanical nature. To his parents' horror he even dismantled their prized grandfather clock, had the works scattered all over the floor before they caught him, and then put it all back together again. Much to their surprise, it worked better than it ever had.

Not yet old enough to obtain a driver's license, Jim built his own automobile, a four-wheel coaster with a quarter-horsepower washing machine engine, and he assembled a crystal radio set in a cigar box that brought in stations from distant points. He was an inveterate tinkerer as a child, but no one ever considered the possibility that he might transform that interest into a career.

There was an excellent reason for that thinking. Jim's father was Dr. Thomas Sloan, one of the town's most successful dentists, and his grandfather, Dr. John Sloan, had been another of the area's most prominent dentists. With that sort of a family history, there was no question in anybody's mind that young James would be anything other than a dentist. Jim had no reason to fight the idea—his father and grandfather were highly respected members of the community, they did well financially, and they were able to enjoy all the benefits of working for *themselves*. He applied himself diligently and, in a few years, became James Sloan, D.D.S., with his own office filled with all the latest shining dental equipment. His neighbors called him "Doctor," and he had all the patients he could handle.

But something was happening to Dr. Sloan as his practice continued to grow with each passing year, something he was unable to put his finger on for several years. He was no longer happy about attracting new patients because he was unhappy about the prospect of bending over people in his chair every day, peering into their mouths. He first thought the problem was simply a case of unprofessional boredom and then he recognized that he actually found the whole procedure downright distasteful. He was desperately unhappy and found his only escape was in fixing the mechanical equipment in his office rather than the molars and bicuspids of his patients.

Fortunately, James Sloan was an industrious man who realized that work was important to his mental well-being. After much agonizing he decided to seek the help of a vocational guidance professional. This was something he had never done before because neither he nor anyone who knew him had ever considered the possibility that he would not make a superb dentist. The batteries of aptitude and vocational-interest tests only confirmed what he had known all his life: his real interests were in machines and things mechanical. Spurred on by the guidance counselor, the erstwhile dentist did the first really creative thinking about work in his life. He was then en route to wealth and happiness in an enterprise he enjoyed.

In retrospect, the solution to James Sloan's work problem seemed ludicrously simple, even to him. He abandoned his practice and used his assets to open a first-rate dental laboratory that became enormously successful supplying the dentists in his state with all their needs. He became the master mechanic he had always longed to be, especially qualified because of all the knowledge, skills, and experience garnered during his years as a practicing dentist. He became an achiever because he was not content merely to make a good living in a job that left him feeling frustrated and inadequate.

Is a Career Change Worth the Risk?

Volunteering to relinquish a secure, well-paying job to enter a new career in a society where the little $5,000 car and the $100,000 starter home seem to be outmoded is a step that demands careful thinking, even among the most confident. On the other hand, those who are not living up to their presumed potential will eventually have no choice in the matter. Today many organizations request early retirement and sometimes terminate those employees whom they look upon as being "dead wood." The achiever will make things happen *for* him rather than waiting for them to happen *to* him.

There is no good reason for anyone today, with a college education that was designed to give him special training for success in a particular field, to discover later that he's completely lost in a job that he's accepted in that area. He should have determined his aptitude for the work during his college days. However, if he sees that he is not living up to his own expectations or to those of his boss, he would be wise to take a new look at the personal qualities that had made him believe he would be a success in the first place. Defeat, like victory, is often the result of something small enough to be overlooked, and changing failure into success is the ultimate satisfaction.

The confident individual thinks in terms of *waste*

rather than risk. Consider the lives of two of the greatest leaders in American history. Although they lived in different times, both grew to manhood in the same general area of the country. Neither had the advantage of wealth or a fine education, but both wanted to "be a success" and dedicated themselves to lives of achievement. Both men were gregarious and at ease talking with their neighbors and thought they could best use those talents to prosper as shopkeepers. Each opened a store, and each business failed miserably. Yet, neither man let failure deter him, and each later found an even more demanding calling in which he could put his abilities to greater use—politics. Each man was elected president of the United States and saw the nation through times of great peril.

Risk? Think of the *waste* if *Abraham Lincoln had been a great success as an Illinois grocer and if Harry Truman had really made a go of it as a Kansas City haberdasher!*

Do-It-Yourself or the Corporate Ladder?

For the most part, the old idea of following in your father's footsteps has gone the way of the village blacksmith. In recent years, many of our brightest and most enterprising young men and women have decided to become entrepreneurs right after college or within a very few years after graduation, passing up an opportunity to begin in a large organization or in a profession for which many of them were educated.

The success of so many of these people proves that entrepreneurship is a valid option, although one not devoid of great risk. An article in the October 1985 issue of *Success Magazine,* published in Harlan, Iowa, notes that starting your own business has become something of a craze on college campuses. It verifies that entrepreneurship can be anybody's game and that success knows no age, sex, or ethnic barriers.

Success Magazine quotes Verne Harnish, a twenty-six-year-old former engineering student who has become the national director of the Association of Collegiate Entrepreneurs. Harnish helped found the organization a few years ago in the basement of a Chinese restaurant located in Harvard Square. Here's what he had to say about this new option for eager achievers:

> There are probably three reasons why enthusiasm about entrepreneurship has suddenly sprung up in so many places. First, the technological change from heavy industry to computers and service industries has made it more feasible for young people to get started in their own businesses. Recent graduates can't very well go out and begin building tractors or ships. But they can start a software company or a pizza delivery service.
>
> Second, the recession left a lot of students short of money and looking for jobs. It stimulated some people. If you can't find a job in a big company, maybe you can go out and create your own.
>
> Third, the example of other successful young people has made students think they can succeed as well. Stephen Jobs, co-founder of Apple Computers and now worth more than $10 million, has been a

role model for many people. But there are dozens of others who have served as inspirations.

No matter how you slice it, the business world must look up to these young people. They have indicated they possess the kind of intelligence, industry, and determination that has made them bona fide achievers *today*, rather than in the nebulous future. Few of them inherited wealth, and most worked long and hard to come by their financing. More than any group, these young people typify the modern version of success: the Horatio Algers of the 1980s.

But is going it alone a viable alternative to taking a good job with a big company? That, of course, depends very much on *you* and the kind of personality, character, and knowledge you bring to the workplace. It is a decision that requires the most careful consideration because it may well be the most important one you will ever make in your life.

Peter Drucker, one of America's leading management thinkers and the author of nineteen books on management problems, considered the pros and cons of starting a business in an interview with editors of *Inc.* magazine in Los Angeles.

The great majority of small businesses are incapable of innovation, partly because they don't have the resources, but a lot more because they don't have the time and they don't have the ambition. . . . Look at the typical small business. It's grotesquely understaffed. It doesn't have the resources or the cash flow. . . . [The owner] is basically fighting the daily battle. He doesn't have, by and large, the discipline. He doesn't have the background. The most successful of the young entrepreneurs today are people who have spent five to eight years in a big organization.

They learn. They get tools. They learn to do a cash-flow analysis and how one trains people and how one delegates and how one builds a team. The ones without that background are the entrepreneurs who, no matter how great their success, are being pushed out. For example, if you ask me what's wrong with Wozniak and Jobs, the co-founders of Apple Computer, Inc., they don't have the discipline. They don't have the tools, the knowledge.

Mr. Drucker was referring to the ouster of Mr. Jobs, the chairman of Apple Computer, from day-to-day responsibilities in the management. Jobs later resigned as chairman and confounded everyone by announcing that he was planning to start a rival computer company, although he was still the largest individual stockholder in Apple. Mr. Drucker went on to say:

The Lord was singularly unkind to them [Wozniak and Jobs]. By giving them too much success too soon. If the Lord wants to destroy, He does what He did to those two. They never got their noses rubbed in the dirt. They never had to dig. It came too easy. Success made them arrogant. They don't know the simple elements. They're like an architect who doesn't know how one drives a nail or what a stud is.

It is readily apparent that Mr. Drucker believes that any aspiring entrepreneur could better prepare himself for the rigors of active management by getting his feet wet with a large organization. There is much to be said for that viewpoint, provided you are relatively happy with the work and consider it a learning experience. After several years of absorbing real management technique, you will be better equipped to make an informed decision either to concentrate on moving up the corporate ladder or to start your own enterprise.

Young people, like those who started Apple Computer, are to be admired because the rewards come only to those who dare. At the same time, the story of their difficulties is not unusual. The innovation and zeal that launch a new company like a rocket often fizzle because the young entrepreneurs simply lack the long-range experience that could prepare them for future difficulties. Sadly, the casualty rate among new high-tech companies has been as high as seven or eight out of every ten new starts.

A Budding New Concept

The smashing successes that some young entrepreneurs have managed to achieve has not gone unnoticed by the major American companies. These companies have long thrived on the infusions of new blood and enthusiasm from the college campuses, and they are not happy seeing it channeled off into new directions. As a direct result, a new word has been added to the vocabulary of business: *intrapreneur.*

*Intra*preneurs are carefully monitored employees of

a corporation who have demonstrated special entrepreneurial ambitions and talents. Their risks of failure are greatly reduced because they are encouraged to stay and start up their new enterprises *within* the company. Both the company and the employee benefit because the company acquires an innovative new business while the idea man avoids financial concern.

This is a *new* concept that promises to widen the horizons of those determined to be leaders. It has already been adopted by a number of U.S. companies on an experimental basis, and it seems likely to spread. Think of the grand new opportunities—companies reorganizing and becoming a confederation of entrepreneurs operating under the corporation's name. This is an exciting new opening for the achiever: *intrapreneurialism.*

All of the emerging new opportunities in America's free-enterprise system make it all the more promising for anyone with a willingness to work hard and a strong drive to succeed. This makes it all the more important that you select a career that truly interests you, one that continually challenges you to do your best work—the *right work.*

THE BOTTOM LINE

1. Even the most disciplined individual will find it virtually impossible to advance in work that fails to excite him.

2. Challenge and opportunity for advancement

will be ultimately more important than starting salary for those entering the work force.

3. The risks are great, but creative thinking and determination have made millionaires of many who have started their own businesses.

4. Most experts agree that several years of on-the-job training with a big company make a venture into entrepreneurism much safer.

5. Investigate the possibility of your parent company's sponsoring you in a venture in intrapreneurism.

4

COMMENCEMENT: THE BEGINNING OF LEARNING

The whole object of education is, or should be, to develop the mind. The mind should be a thing that works. It should be able to pass judgement on events as they arise, make decisions.
—SHERWOOD ANDERSON

There was a time, not too many years ago, when the lack of a college degree was no great impediment to a natively intelligent individual who had a burning desire to succeed. Outside the very specialized professions—law, medicine, and so on—a college degree tended to open more doors, but it was not necessarily a prerequisite for success. Today, when increasing numbers of would-be achievers are investing in postgraduate degrees, the person lacking a bachelor's degree is distinctly handicapped.

Yet, as the eminent playwright Anderson noted, true education is a never-ending process that perpetually develops the mind. There is obviously much truth in the plaintive cry that is raised across the United States in any period of economic decline, "You're nothing today unless you've got a degree." But those with degrees, and those still striving to obtain them, must remember that ongoing education—through special courses, night schools, and so forth—is a must for anyone dedicated to achieving a position of leadership in American business. Those who ignore the dictum "It's never too late to learn" are doomed to a long, uphill climb.

To be flamboyantly alliterative: learning leads to leadership. As Vance Packard, the distinguished sociologist and author points out, there is no hereditary system of nobility in America as there is in England and elsewhere. There never has been one since George Washington put an end to that possibility by declining an offer to become king of this fledgling republic in April 1782. We recognize no legal class distinctions in this nation. Those who do emerge as the wielders of power and influence and the collectors of material wealth have risen to their positions on the basis of personal achievement. Today's achievers—in business, law, medicine, science, and the arts—for the most part got where they are through education and more education.

The world is going through a technological revolution that makes education far more necessary to success today than it was even twenty years ago. The total of accumulated knowledge is doubling every ten years! Only those who make a concerted effort to keep up with this explosion in knowledge have any chance of taking full advantage of it. Even the most gifted individual who walks away from education in his eagerness to make a mark in the "real world" will find that he's facing almost insurmountable competition. There are more college graduates in the United States today than there were high school graduates thirty years ago and, in another few years, there may be as many graduates with advanced degrees as there are holders of baccalaureate degrees today.

James H. Evans, chairman of the Union Pacific Corporation, put the modern education-industrial picture in clearer focus during a talk with students at Texas Christian University:

> Although Americans do tend to have a great respect for education, we also have a certain historical scorn for the academic community. We have plenty of Horatio Algers in our midst who have made it without the benefit of a college education. It was, after all, one of our greatest industrialists, Andrew Carnegie, who once observed, with a certain amount of relish, that there was an "almost total absence of college graduates from high positions in the business world."

> There may be some with similar feelings today, but I would submit to them that times have changed and are changing even more. Knowledge has grown exponentially, and worldwide competition has become fierce. Mr. Carnegie's steel mills did not have to compete with those of Japan, Korea, and Brazil. His labor force was composed largely of recent European immigrants, and they worked long

hours at low wages. The managers of his mills didn't worry much about effluents, EPA standards, OSHA or equal employment opportunity.

The grades of ore that were mined in the United States were richer and more easily accessible in his time. And the steel industry didn't face vigorous competition from alternative materials such as plastics and aluminum. If Mr. Carnegie were around today, trying to stay afloat in the steel industry, I know he would be surrounded by college graduates to help him deal with these complex problems.

Clearly we need educated people, and we need educated people of all types. We need engineers, economists, scientists and managers to help rejuvenate our manufacturing industries. We need computer scientists to help build new knowledge industries and help modernize older ones. We need geologists and engineers to propel and maintain our energy industries. And we need medical, natural and physical scientists to continue to expand the frontiers of knowledge.

At Union Pacific, as at most corporations, before we make a new investment, we very carefully calculate our probable rate of return on that investment. Unfortunately, it is not possible to make that kind of calculation with educational expenditures. Yet, we do know that, in the aggregate, education is the kind of investment that has tremendous leverage. It can excite minds in ways that will produce yields that dwarf the investment. (quoted in *Forbes Scrapbook*)

Mr. Evans, a man dealing with the practical, everyday challenges of business, minces no words in clarifying the importance that he and other industrial leaders place on the value of higher education in today's job market. Fortunately, today it is easier for the average young person to receive college training than it was in bygone days. Financial aid is still available in the form of scholarships, student loans, and government grants. Much of the same financial help can be had by those seeking professional and advanced degrees. Attempting to rush into a career today without the advantages of a good education is the finite example of "putting the cart before the horse."

Are Those Without College Degrees Doomed to Failure?

Not at all! Even those who have been performing well in the corporate structure but are disheartened because others with better educations (but no more ability) have been passing them by should not be prepared to wave the white flag. There are too many options that can increase their worth available. Although the situation has grown more complex in recent years, the simple truth is that *it's never too late to learn.* Consider the case of a man named Hogan.

Jack Hogan (not his real name) was one of nine children born to a poor, but hardworking Irish-American family in Boston a number of years ago when opportunity was much harder to find than it is today. His parents had difficulty earning enough money even to feed their nine children, let alone send them to high school. College was only for the offspring of the rich and powerful. At that time the children had to contribute to the family income when they were old enough, and, when Jack reached the age of fourteen, his mother took him on the streetcar to downtown Boston to look for suitable employment. His obvious brightness and good manners earned him a job in the first place they visited, the employment office of a large bank. Jack became a bank office boy at a salary of *eight dollars a week.*

Jack Hogan was promoted to clerk after several years of hard work, but he was then old enough to realize that he was never going to go much higher in the banking business without further education. He was certain that would be true in the city of Boston, generally recognized as the educational capital of America. His ability to learn and his willingness to take on extra work were recognized by a thoughtful older man in the Personnel Department who alerted him to a possible solution to his dilemma. The bank had just introduced a new program of evening classes designed to help ambitious young employees further their education at a local college, at the bank's expense.

That was all the encouragement Jack Hogan needed. He would be starting at a lower position than others because he didn't even have a high school diploma, but he applied for admission and won acceptance. It took him ten long years of after-hours study, but Jack earned his high school diploma, a bachelor of arts degree, and finally his law degree. Impressed by his ambition, persistence, and hard work, the bank promoted him again and again during and after his period of night classes. Jack Hogan literally transformed his dreams of success into reality, and before he retired, at age sixty-five, he held the post of executive vice-president of a great metropolitan bank.

Education Must Be an Ongoing Process

The ceremonies in which degrees are conferred at a college or university are known as commencement. That word, *commencement,* takes on special meaning for anyone intent on reaching special heights. The new graduate is commencing his journey away from the shelter of academia and into real life, and the ambitious will be starting a lifelong process of learning through practical experience and many more formal courses of study. This attitude, that education is a lifetime process, is especially valid today when the careers of American businessmen take them to Europe, Asia, Latin America, and all stops between.

Roger Buckworth (not his real name) is a young man who had great success because he recognized that education must not stop at commencement. Roger was graduated from an excellent four-year liberal-arts college in Iowa, his home state. He was a serious student and made fine marks in a host of courses in American and English literature, history, science and mathematics, and philosophy. His was the traditional liberal education designed to make him a well-rounded person, suitable for positions of responsibility in any number of occupations. To his delight, Roger was eagerly recruited by the Ajax Corporation, where he accepted a position immediately after graduation.

However, Ajax was a company with widespread interests in Latin America, and Roger quickly recognized that there was one flaw in his education that could slow his progress at Ajax. If he was going to get anywhere with the company, he would have to speak and understand Spanish, a language with which he was completely unfamiliar. He was not about to allow that inadequacy to deter him, and he began scouting around for help.

He found what he was looking for at a nearby university. The school offered classes in Spanish grammar and conversation every evening between five and seven. That schedule dovetailed neatly with his working hours, and he actually found the learning of a second language interesting and challenging. He enjoyed it so much he began listening to Spanish-language programs on radio and television and even subscribed to *La Prensa,* a daily Hispanic newspaper. He was confident his outside study would pay off eventually, and he made certain his personnel file contained a detailed accounting of his new skills.

The break he was hoping for came a few years later when an important executive position in the company opened up in Caracas, Venezuela. It was Ajax policy to fill significant positions from within the company, whenever possible, and the top brass narrowed the selection process down to four promising candidates, including Roger Buckworth. One candidate was especially well qualified, and the other three were close behind. However, of the four, only Roger was capable of speaking and writing Spanish fluently and also possessed a real interest in and knowledge of the people and their customs. His "long-shot scheme"—actually intelligent planning—paid off and Roger got the job and a ticket to bigger and better things.

The story of Roger Buckworth illustrates that possession of a valid college degree often is not enough to secure the kind of success desired by those intent on achieving the most. It also demonstrates that real help is available for those who don't even have degrees. In this era of specialization, many extremely capable men and women have done very well on the strength of a liberal-arts education that provided them with a sound cultural background. But think a moment of the greater strength they would have had if they had continued their formal education by taking advantage of available courses in specific areas that were either not required or offered while they were in school.

This is a very special time of almost unlimited opportunity in America for those willing both to learn and to work, no matter how humble their origins or how limited their financial resources. The really vital resources are intelligence, determination, and a willingness to learn. In most countries of the world, even today, it is often almost impossible to break free from the class into which you were born. Not so in America.

Education is a most important element in today's equation for success. But so is a simple truth that too many people tend to overlook: *It is never too late to go back to school or to get more schooling, no matter how old you are!*

THE BOTTOM LINE

1. The total of accumulated knowledge is doubling every ten years, making it imperative that every leader keep abreast of this information revolution.

2. Time spent acquiring a postgraduate degree in a field in which it is deemed vital should be considered a sound investment.

3. Thoroughly investigate the possibility of enrolling in any and all educational programs that may be sponsored by your employer.

4. Liberal-arts graduates can increase their value to the company and to themselves by taking courses in the applicable, more specialized subjects that were not a part of their college curriculum.

5. With the widespread availability of evening classes, extension courses, and various forms of financial aid for education, there is ample opportunity for everyone to better his or her position in the information revolution.

5

USE HABITS AS *DECISION ELIMINATORS*

Nothing so needs reforming as other people's habits.
—MARK TWAIN

From the time we get up in the morning until the moment we go to sleep at night, most of our actions are controlled by habit. Unfortunately, as Mark Twain implies, many of these habits become destructive to us and downright unpleasant to our associates. In a business situation bad habits can also prove to be highly unprofitable.

Dr. Samuel Johnson, the English lexicographer and critic, said some two hundred years ago: "The chains of habit are too weak to be felt until they are too strong to be broken." Tryon Edwards, as quoted in *Forbes Scrapbook*, described bad habits in similar terms: "Any act often repeated forms a habit; and habit allowed, steadily gains in strength. At first it may be but as the spider's web, easily broken through, but if not resisted it soon binds us with chains of steel."

With such criticism directed against them, are *all* habits necessarily bad? I think not. If you had to spend time each morning in an inner debate on the awesome subject of which sock to put on first or whether to have only toast and coffee or eggs and bacon for breakfast, how much time could you spend thinking about the important things waiting in the day ahead? The fact is, we couldn't survive the day if we had to make a conscious decision every step of the way. The right kinds of habits are indispensable to daily living.

It has often been said that man is "just a bundle of habits," and there's no doubt that the bad habits have a way of attracting more attention than the good. Because habits play such important roles in our lives, it follows that we can profit by gaining a better understanding of the way they are formed and the ways they can be abused—or *used.* Instead of becoming slaves to our habits, it behooves us to make slaves of our habits.

The beginning step in this process might be to view habits in a new and more positive light. In a very real sense, habits can be utilized as *decision eliminators.* They can do for you what the automatic pilot does for the captain of an airliner on a transcontinental flight: free you to concentrate on more immediate matters. This doesn't mean you should use your automatic pilot (habit) on takeoffs, in emergency situations, or on landings, but it can prove to be a trustworthy ally if it's been programmed to function properly.

Psychologists have carefully analyzed the way in which habits are formed and this is the way it works. The *sensory nerves* bring a message from the senses— that is, vision, hearing, touch, taste, and smell—to the brain. The brain makes a conscious decision as the result of this input and quickly sends the appropriate order through the *motor nerves* to the proper parts of the body, commanding certain action. After the same reaction to identical stimuli occurs twenty-five or thirty times, the need for a conscious decision by the brain is eliminated and the reaction becomes automatic. In other words, *a habit has been formed.* Because of repetition, the message from the sensory nerve jumps across to the proper motor nerve without a conscious decision by the brain.

Remember, you will normally form a habit when this bypass action takes place twenty-five or thirty times. If you consciously decide to brush your teeth immediately upon rising and do this for twenty-five to thirty consecutive mornings, you form a very beneficial habit. If you fail to follow this regular routine faithfully, you leave yourself open to chance, and that can be the start of a *bad* habit.

Why this lengthy, detailed, and somewhat elementary explanation? To make a point: *Conscious repetition of an action over a period of time makes that action a habit. If you can consciously form a good habit, you can also consciously reverse the process to eliminate a bad habit!* As simplistic as this statement sounds, it is a scientifically proven fact. Most of our good habits, usually referred to as fine character traits, are a modus operandi instilled into us by our parents and teachers or efforts we have consciously made to improve ourselves. Most bad habits are negatives that creep into our lives without conscious effort. It is now clear that we have strong biological aids that can help us correct those bad habits, and this is good news, indeed.

You Can Change Your Life by Changing Your Habits

Study the biography of any great achiever and it is immediately evident that he or she was a person capable of exercising enormous self-discipline. It is this ability to harness strengths and minimize weaknesses that enabled these people to bring the maximum effort to their work and ease the way to the summit. But how did they get that way? How is it possible for the normal individual, not blessed with superhuman strength, to go about changing his habits?

It is first necessary to identify these actions that so influence our lives. After all, we couldn't overcome the force of gravity until the legendary apple conked old Isaac's noggin, proving its existence. Try to make an inventory of your habits, both the good and the bad. You'll have to be scrupulously honest in considering your bad habits (you may have to enlist the help of family and close friends) because the insidious, involuntary nature of bad habits often keeps them hidden from us. If you can succeed in actually listing all of your habits, you will be well on your way to making them work *for* you rather than against you.

Author Somerset Maugham made this droll but

true observation: "The unfortunate thing about this world is that good habits are so much easier to give up than bad ones." That goes along with the thinking that "Everything I enjoy is either illegal, immoral, or fattening!" Giving up your bad habits, especially those that have been a part of you for a long time, will not be easy. But the fact that so many are succeeding proves that it can be done, and your individual future dictates that it must be done. The bottom line is that no one can do it *for* you. Psychologists, therapists, and participants in group sessions will tell you that only powerful, self-motivated action by you will get the job done.

Making It Work

Each individual must ultimately find his own best methods of breaking a bad habit. Walter Richman perfected a method that worked for him and might well point the direction for others to follow. At the age of twenty, Walter was graduated magna cum laude from the business school of his state university. He was near the top of his class, and several of his professors urged him to stay on to study for advanced degrees that would enable him to join their ranks as a teacher.

But during his senior year Walter's continual lack of money forced him to seek part-time work, and he began to sell insurance. He enjoyed the work, decided to stay with it, and, by the time he reached his twenty-fourth birthday, he had been promoted to sales manager of his local office. His business-school training, personality, and ambition transformed a "part-time job" into a satisfying and profitable career. By all standards Walter should have been heading for the top.

However, within a few years, Walter recognized that he had a serious problem, one that was damaging his health. It was a time when the American public was being bombarded, in every area of the media, to "relax and have a cigarette." In his position as sales manager Walter was dealing with people, employees and clients, and their problems, all day long, and the stress of the situation began to take its toll on Walter. He did as advised and found himself increasingly "relaxing over a cigarette." It became impossible for him to conduct a meeting without lighting one cigarette after another, and only a persistent cough made him cognizant of the fact that he was now smoking *three packs a day*.

The cough refused to go away, and Walter made the unpleasant discovery that he had become hooked on nicotine. What he had once considered a relaxing break from stress he now recognized as a very destructive habit. He had never seriously considered quitting because smoking had become an ingrained part of his daily ritual. Richman was forced to take stock of himself. The stress of his work had driven him to chain-smoking. Should he find work that was less demanding? The foolishness of that question snapped him back to reality: "Were cigarettes worth losing his job, losing his family, losing his self-respect?"

That same day Walter Richman worked out a verbal agreement with himself, on the same businesslike terms he used in his career. It was a three-part agreement he felt he could keep:

1. He would quit *cold turkey*. There would be *no* exceptions—not one cigarette. He had already tried tapering off and he knew that did not work for him.

2. *Substitution*. He had read in a psychology text that it was beneficial to substitute a harmless habit for a destructive one. He decided to put a Toosie Roll candy bar, the approximate size of a cigarette, between his lips every time he felt the urge for a cigarette. Because smoking is a largely physical habit, the candy gave him something to occupy his mouth and hands.

3. *Not forever*. He wanted to make no promises he couldn't keep, so his total smoking ban would not be forever: to stay on the safe side, he made it for a duration of three months. He was still full of doubts about his solemn bargain, and he told himself he would resume his "enjoyable habit" if he did not see improvements in his health and outlook at the end of three months.

A thoroughly honorable businessman, he was doggedly determined to live up to his agreement with himself. To his surprise, his nagging cough disappeared completely within two weeks and that encouraging success made it easier for him to continue to honor his pledge. Within two *months,* he had gained thirty pounds—another improvement because it brought him up to normal weight for his height and age for the first time in years. He took delight in really tasting his favorite food again and gloried in a newfound energy and enthusiasm for life and work. Best of all, he had the supreme satisfaction of conquering a debilitating bad habit. His "three-month trial" transformed a bad habit into a new lease on life, and he has never looked back.

As countless millions of Americans have learned in

recent years, breaking the smoking habit can be one of the most difficult but rewarding tasks you can undertake. Conquering a serious alcohol or drug problem is an equally inspiring accomplishment. However, if you've invested the necessary effort to read this book on self-management, it's unlikely that you are bothered by such overwhelming afflictions. Let's return to the more basic, niggling little bad habits that can quietly dissipate our good intentions and our goals in life.

Be ruthless with yourself. Find those negative aspects of your personality and write them down. Are you overly defensive—too quick to put the blame for your inadequacies on circumstances or on the incompetence of others? Are you a procrastinator—someone who finds himself continually behind schedule? Are you too self-centered—unwilling to listen to others' opinions? Bad habits like these can ruin our lives and our careers, without our conscious knowledge.

How to Build Good Habits

Because this book is primarily career-oriented, it's a pleasure to report that building good habits on the job is a far easier task than ridding oneself of bad habits. On the other hand, transforming habits into positive decision eliminators will carry over outside the workplace and gradually be a part of your makeup during all your waking hours.

Successful people have formed the habit of doing the things that failures don't like to do.

—ALBERT E. N. GRAY

Consider that thought-provoking statement. Mr. Gray, a top executive of the Prudential Insurance Company, made it many years ago and intended it as a reference to the workplace. But he stressed the word *people* rather than *employees*. In a real sense, doing the things we don't like to do can make us more successful in our social as well as our business lives.

Albert E. N. Gray, with authority over some thirty thousand office workers and salesmen, had reason to come to the conclusion he reached: His primary job was to oversee the motivation and training of Prudential's thousands of employees. He had ample opportunity over the years to study them at first hand, to analyze what made them tick, to pinpoint the differences between the successes and the failures.

The key word in Gray's equation is *habit*, meaning the "things they do" habitually. The successes were the individuals who *habitually* took over the most difficult jobs in the field or office, jobs that others sidestepped or avoided. The failing salesmen had a dread of calling on strangers; the successful salesmen trained themselves to look on it as a challenge. The failing salesmen were usually reluctant to come right out and ask for an order; the successful knew that was the name of the game and attempted to *close* early and often.

When you make a list of your habits, also write down all the duties your job entails and rate yourself on your performance. Again, be ruthless with yourself. Any bright individual who is aware of his strengths and weaknesses, his duties and his actions, is intelligent enough to set them straight. Know yourself. Then make yourself someone *you* can respect.

Dr. Henry C. Link, the eminent Colgate University

psychologist and author, wrote in *Rediscovery of Man*: "The frequent causes of inferiority which we find among people today are due almost entirely to the failure to cultivate specific habits of success."

This puts the ball squarely in our own court. We are all bundles of habits. But within us we have the power to change these habits, to change the habits that lead to failure to the habits that lead to success.

THE BOTTOM LINE

1. Habits are built like muscles in a physical-fitness program: repetition makes them stronger. Routine and time develop them into integral parts of our character.

2. Ask family and close friends to help in identifying the bad habits that are limiting your progress and make a plan to change them.

3. Approach the worst problems with a three-pronged attack: (a) Resolve to stop immediately with no exceptions; (b) substitute an opposite action to replace it; (c) allow yourself a specific period of time in which to succeed.

4. Always bear in mind Albert E. N. Gray's statement, "Successful people have formed the habit of doing the things that failures don't like to do."

6

CREATING A FAVORABLE IMPRESSION

We all want to be at our best when we meet people and most especially when applying for a job, or addressing an audience, or calling on a client, or developing new contacts. It is important for us to feel confident and secure in our appearance and our ability to express ourselves. There are certain skills necessary to "create a favorable impression" whether speaking, writing, creating, or acting.

What does this have to do with being an achiever? A great deal!

For every impression you make on another, there must be some expression on your part. Expression consists of taking all the sterling qualities buried inside you—your intelligence, your charm, your enthusiasm, your quick wit—and making sure that they get *outside* of you to be heard and seen by as many people as possible.

1. *Speaking.* In a personal one-on-one meeting, or in the corporate boardroom, or at the rostrum in a huge auditorium, or on nationwide television, the ability to speak effectively enables us to communicate our worth and to advance our ideas. There are those who say they come across well in private conversations but freeze in a public situation. This limits their opportunities for advancement because today anyone who achieves *must be* a good public speaker.

How can you overcome this lack of confidence in yourself? One of the best methods is to record yourself on tape. This will enable you to ascertain how you sound to others. Listen attentively to yourself and make a conscious effort to note whether you can improve the quality of your voice, your diction, your grammar, your vocabulary, what you have to say and the effectiveness of your delivery. Whether in a small group or a large forum the way you say what you say will have an immeasurable impact on your real chances for success.

2. *Writing.* You may say you cannot write. William Randolph Hearst, the famous newsman and editor, refuted this when he said: "Anyone who can think, can write." As with any other skill the way to express yourself through your writing is to practice, to start writing and keep writing. Achievers have learned to organize their thoughts and ideas and put them down on paper.

Many have written books and magazine articles pertaining to their special interest in their chosen field of endeavor. Without their ability to write they would not have achieved such widespread recognition, Lee Iacocca, George Burns, to name just two.

You may not harbor a secret desire to become an author. However, are you confident that you can write an important report, or even a good interoffice memo, that will be read by the top people of your company? Writing is a basic tool of communication that gives others a strong impression of your value. It also has the added impact of longevity: it can be studied again. Before you go into a meeting, take the time to organize and write down your thoughts. Make a dedicated effort to write your notes clearly. Then when you enter the discussion you will be fluent and concise in putting your ideas across.

3. *Creating.* Creative thinking is inventing. Authors invent plots, characters, scenes, situations. Inventors have given us radio, television, cars, computers. Scientists have opened many new roads to explore in medicine, in space, and in preserving our planet. The authors, the inventors, and the scientists impress the public with their ideas. Creativeness impresses everyone.

The creative worker looks beyond his own perimeter while he performs the duties assigned to him. Many of us do not recognize our creativity but we all have some. If you can develop and project your creativity, you'll have a head start on the person who occupies the office next door.

4. *Acting.* Whatever your line of work may be, you

must also be an *actor*, an individual who projects a constant image of ability and confidence. It's no miracle that President Ronald Reagan was able to win reelection by a landslide and be universally called "The Great Communicator." After all, he was *trained as an actor*. If you want to be recognized as an outstanding head of a department, manager, or chief executive officer, you must be prepared to play the role at all times and to back it up with extensive homework. Acting, in this sense, means you must look the role you have chosen to play, in your personal grooming, your wardrobe, your carriage, and your overall demeanor. Those you work for and with are your audience, an audience composed of critics, judge, and jury, as well as friends and supporters. You may find it relaxing to be sloppy and careless in the privacy of your home, but when you're on that work *stage*, carry yourself as if you were a supremely confident actor making an opening night entrance to thunderous applause.

Spreading the Word

Now when you have mastered the techniques of expression, what do you do with them? What is it you are trying to accomplish? What impression will help you the most?

Aren't you trying to build a reputation? A favorable reputation. A reputation as a leader—a man or woman who gets things done, an achiever.

"The time devoted to earning a good reputation is well spent," says Dr. Leonard Cammer. "Doors open easily for those with a good reputation and opportunities are offered to them that might otherwise be withheld."

Dr. Cammer is a former psychiatry professor at New York Medical College. Based on his clinical experience, Dr. Cammer says that you must first respect yourself or others will never respect you. You must avoid false humility. Don't pretend you're not very good at something you do very well; people resent false humility because they feel it is really a device to invite compliments. On the other hand, don't be afraid to admit it when you don't know something; people respect those who have enough self-confidence to admit both their strengths and their weaknesses. Always honor all commitments to others and accept your obligations willingly. These attitudes command the respect of others.

A favorable reputation must be built on sound achievement. Sound achievement is the sine qua non, the indispensable factor, the foundation on which to build sound personal public relations. Without it, any reputation is built on sand. There is a definition of public relations that should never be forgotten: "Public relations is 90 percent doing a good job and 10 percent getting credit for it." Nothing will convince the public or your peers of your worth if it is obvious that you have done a poor job.

Although there are professional firms eager to promote your public image, you should always "mastermind" your personal public relations program. You must adroitly have other people "sing your praises." To sing your own praises will label you as a braggart and a self-promoter. This is the opposite of the impression you wish to create. There are more subtle ways of putting over the story of your abilities. You may not realize it, but your immediate world is full of voluntary publicists who appreciate your abilities and accomplishments and would be eager to help you. These are your friends, neighbors, and colleagues. When the right occasion arises, give them a copy of your biographical sketch or a newspaper clipping, make them privy to your new success. People love to talk about the importance of their friends to others. They want their other friends to know how important you are. Your success builds up their own importance, that anyone as successful as you would be their friend.

Frank Hepplewhite (not his real name) had an outstanding career as a lawyer in the South. He had been president of the city bar association and the state bar association. A tax and corporation lawyer, Frank had won some fierce court battles saving some of the most important corporations in his state millions of dollars.

Frank had always been active in the alumni group of his alma mater and had served as national president of his alumni association. He was a longtime trustee of a prestigious hospital. He had been appointed by the governor of his state to head up several fact-finding commissions that saved the state millions of dollars and lowered the tax rate.

A few of his friends knew of some of his accomplishments but none of them knew of *all* of the positions he had held and all the honors he had received. They read them for the first time when they read his biographical sketch, which his firm updated from time to time and distributed to prospective clients.

As soon as his friends knew more about his achievements, everybody in his city knew about them and was singing his praises.

You may have a high degree of intelligence, a winning personality, and the ability to get things done. You may know you have these qualities, but until others know you have them you will never be known as an achiever.

One of the most effective ways, and the most satisfying way, of becoming favorably known is to form the habit of helping others to attain *their* goals without any thought of personal benefit to yourself.

If you go out of your way to help someone get into the college of his choice or help someone to land the job he so badly needs to advance his career, he will never forget what you have done for him, and although you gave your help freely and with no thought whatsoever of being repaid for your efforts, the beneficiary of your kindness will become one of your greatest centers of influence.

You belong to an organization and like most organizations yours is always looking for the right kind of new members.

In visiting with an acquaintance you find out he would very much like to join your organization. He fits the description of the kind of new member the organization is looking for. You offer to put him up for membership.

You have accomplished two things: you have added a desirable new member, and you have made a friend of an acquaintance, a friend who will never forget what you have done for him and will become one of your most powerful publicists.

Some day, maybe several years later, you will discover that an unusual opportunity that has come your way came as a result of what you did for your friend.

You Are Your Most Important Product

1. Study the people at the top, where you aim to be one day. The achievers, the leaders, almost without exception, immediately put you at ease when you meet them. The bigger they are, the easier they are to meet and converse with; top leaders make a habit of being gracious and being helpful.

2. Appearance is a vital component in the overall image you project. As the great plastic surgeon Maxwell Maltz discovered, an improvement in a patient's appearance quickly changed his image of himself and increased his self-esteem. Achievers always stand out in attitude and appearance. They recognize the importance of fine-quality clothes and the time spent on careful grooming. If you have an inclination to think of clothing as little more than a frivolous display of materialism, you should consider this fact: until recent years the New York headquarters of many major companies insisted that their staff members comply with a rigid *dress code.* A nationally known New York accounting firm permitted its employees to wear nothing but *white* shirts with their suits and ties well into the 1980s. Such dress codes have been relaxed today, thanks in great part to the influx of women into the upper echelons of business. Women, all too aware that they would have to do battle with ingrained sexism, quickly learned the advantages of "dressing for success." That's a lesson that too many ambitious young men tend to overlook against a background of today's casual nonworking life-styles.

3. Younger people just starting out with little surplus money are sometimes reluctant to buy really good clothes, thinking no one will know the difference. There is no mistake as injurious to your image as wearing poor-quality clothing. When you think you don't have the money to buy expensive clothes, do it anyway. You will be betting on yourself, betting that you are going to be a success. Your clothes are an investment in yourself. Often they are the first impression someone forms of you as you enter a room. As the cover of a book may or may not give us a true indication of the worth of its content, it certainly can make us pause and think about it. Your clothes are like the cover of a book.

If you think that only you know how little you pay for your clothing, ask yourself this question: Would I feel equally secure about my appearance if each suit I owned carried the price tag on the lapel where everyone could see it?

4. While you are spending your money investing in your future, don't overlook entertaining. People enjoy invitations to lunch or to dine in a fine restaurant or in your home. This provides an opportunity for you to become better acquainted under favorable circumstances.

5. Creating a favorable impression is your personal

public relations program. It must be done with great finesse. Give it a lot of thought. A small investment of time and money in your personal public relations could come back to you a hundredfold.

THE BOTTOM LINE

1. You can improve your speaking ability by tape-recording your voice and studying it. Be conscious of your weaknesses in grammar, vocabulary, and diction. Select a public figure whose speaking you admire and attempt to emulate him.

2. Constant practice will strengthen your writing skills. Learn to put your thoughts on paper in a concise, uncomplicated style that will make you a more effective writer and public speaker.

3. If you think of yourself as an *actor*, you will remember that you are always "on stage" and must remain within the character you have written for yourself. Dress for the part and allow others to enjoy the successful person you hope to be.

4. Almost every fashion expert agrees that a really successful businessman's wardrobe should consist of several basic suits. Choose your shoes and accessories carefully and never shortchange yourself on quality. Dress for your way of life and invest in your future.

5. Up-and-coming women executives hardly need fashion advice from this corner. In a male-dominated work environment, a woman should dress in a manner that clearly demonstrates her businesslike attitude without downgrading her femininity.

6. Your personal public relations program must begin with a willingness to share your success with friends and associates. Tact and subtlety are the key elements, and it's always wiser to induce others to spread the news of your accomplishments. Be considerate at all times. There are only two kinds of manners—good and bad. Be sure that yours are good!

7. Creating a favorable impression is but the first step in the long process of establishing a good reputation. This action should not be confined to the job and must continue after office hours out in the community. Get *involved.*

7

MAKE ENTHUSIASM YOUR PARTNER

There is no other quality that attracts people to us more than enthusiasm. Enthusiastic people radiate a joy in what they do and they make us want to participate in their activities. Their attitude motivates us to get the show on the road. Enthusiasm is a vital component for success.

—THE AUTHOR

It was three o'clock on a February afternoon in Florida in 1985 in an auditorium filled to overflowing. J. Peter Grace, short, stocky, and bouncy, stood on the speaker's platform, holding his audience riveted to their seats, urging them to join with him and with two hundred other top executives from all over America to stop government waste.

Peter Grace, chief executive of W. R. Grace & Company, had been selected by President Reagan to head up the President's Private Sector Survey on Cost

Control. The president's orders were to search for waste and inefficiency in the federal government. Mr. Grace's committee, composed of top business executives and 2,000 or more volunteers from across the land, examined the government's operations in relation to cost control for eighteen months. They came up with 2,478 ways to cut waste and increase revenues in order to reduce the federal deficit.

"We must blow the whistle on government waste! There's no need to cut back on government services. Just halt the government spending by Congress," Grace stated in no uncertain terms.

The minute this man of small stature spoke he became a big man. With his energy, his force, his great enthusiasm, he immediately won his audience. They never relaxed and never sat back in their chairs until his final words.

His performance was all the more remarkable because he had left Tokyo the night before at midnight to fly to the afternoon meeting in Florida.

Grace, at age seventy-one, still presides over the successful operation of Grace & Company, whose sales have increased from $350 million to $7.5 billion under his leadership. In addition, he is the chairman of several hospitals and heads many national charitable organizations. He is without doubt one of the busiest men in America and one of its great achievers.

His strong convictions and his great enthusiasm for whatever he is doing have made him the success he is and have attracted many people to his causes.

Enthusiasm is a personality trait you will find in most top leaders in commerce, industry, government, the professions—in every walk of life. It is such a common characteristic of successful people that it cannot be overlooked as one of the principal factors contributing to their success.

As you observe these achievers in action, they give the impression of being habitually enthusiastic about their jobs and everything they undertake. They have cultivated the habit of enthusiasm, as others have cultivated the habit of early rising or saving money or being punctual for appointments.

Consider, for instance, the story of William E. Simon, former secretary of the Treasury of the United States, and now president of the John M. Olin Foundation. Bill Simon's career began in Wall Street where he spent twenty-one years, much of it as a bond salesman. He rose to be one of seven partners of Salomon Brothers, in charge of the Government and Municipal Securities Department. This experience brought him to the attention of Washington and led to his appointment as deputy secretary of the Treasury in January 1973. Later that year, the Mid East oil embargo led to his being named administrator of the Federal Energy Office, a job he handled so well he became the sixty-third secretary of the Treasury in 1974.

Since Bill Simon started his career selling bonds and because our capitalist system has been so good to him, he has become a salesman of the free-enterprise system. Here's what he has to say:

> The capitalist system is an extraordinarily efficient machine that has conferred unprecedented wealth on its adherents, wealth that has liberated countless millions from poverty and the daily grind of just keeping body and soul together. Capitalism is also

the system that best supports democracy. An economic order founded upon respect for individual market decisions and property rights against encroachment by the state.

He concluded by saying, "There in a nutshell, is my sales pitch for the free-market system. It's a pitch I have been making fervently from Wall Street to the Treasury Department, and through my book, *A Time for Truth.*"

Both Peter Grace and Bill Simon are convincing salesmen, salesmen of ideas. And much of their success is due to their enthusiastic presentation of their ideas.

Successful selling and enthusiasm have become synonymous. It would be hard to imagine a calm, cold, or indifferent person as a successful salesman. But quite often the importance of an enthusiastic attitude in other vocations is missed or disregarded. We may think of salesmen only as men and women carrying order books and sample cases, but everyone whose success depends on getting along with people must be a salesman and must play the part of the salesman many times each day.

Although many are unaware of the fact, each one of us is selling himself; the doctor must sell himself to his patients, the college professor to his students, the minister to his congregation, the political jobholder to his constituents. In the business world, the shop- or office worker must sell himself to his superior; and the "boss," if he is to be really effective, must sell himself and his ideas to all those with whom he works.

In this job of selling yourself nothing succeeds like enthusiasm. This one trait is certainly not all that is needed, but many place it near the top of the list of qualities that lead to success.

Enthusiasm like that displayed by Peter Grace, Bill Simon, and so many achievers is something with which only a few are born. Fortunately it can be cultivated and made a part of your personality. Psychologists tell us that most personality traits are acquired; that we are born with some characteristics, but that most of them can be changed; that, to a large extent, we can mold our own personalities.

At this point, you may say to yourself, "These people had something about which they could get enthusiastic. What is there in my job or my life to stir up any enthusiasm?" The answer is that many of these successful leaders developed the habit of being enthusiastic long before they became successful and often attribute to it much of their ability to lead and inspire others.

As already noted, forming any good habit takes time and perseverance. It also calls for some kind of a plan or procedure.

If you feel that your lack of enthusiasm is holding you back in your work or in your contacts with others, here are two suggestions that may help you to make it a full-fledged partner in your daily activities.

How Do I Get It?

Before you can begin to be enthusiastic about anything, you must first sell yourself on its merits and desirability. You cannot be full of negative thoughts and brimming over with enthusiasm at the same time.

The first step, then, is to develop the right habits of thinking, the proper control of your mental attitude. Start by recognizing that nothing in this world is ever perfect or imperfect in the absolute sense. You must almost always weigh the advantages and disadvantages of several courses of action in the light of your objective, and then decide in favor of the action that will advance your furthest toward your goal.

Once you have decided, you must forget about the other things you might have done. Furthermore, you must disregard the obstacles and ignore the difficulties in what you are doing.

In selling yourself, you should adopt the techniques of the salesman. If a real estate salesman were trying to sell you a house, he most certainly would emphasize all its good features and he most assuredly would not call your attention to any of its bad points. You must use this same technique in selling yourself and keeping yourself sold. Think only of the advantages and deliberately ignore the disadvantages.

Some cynics may ridicule this as Pollyanna-type thinking (Pollyanna was an irrepressible optimist), but it is also just common sense. If you have decided that a certain course of action is the only thing to do, then you would be foolish indeed to let *any* thoughts of doubt or discouragement undermine your faith and hope for the plan and destroy your enthusiasm for it.

Act Enthusiastic

In the privacy of your own mind you may be very enthusiastic, but if you give no outward signs of your enthusiasm, no one will ever know you have it. Since most of the power of enthusiasm stems from the effect it has on other people, your enthusiasm must in some way be transmitted to others. The people around you must be made aware of your enthusiasm.

To accomplish this, you must not only be enthusiastic but you must *act* enthusiastic! Let yourself be carried away by forgetting your dignity for a moment and releasing those restraints and inhibitions you have been building up for years. Simply be yourself. Do the things that people do when they are very enthusiastic. Move a little faster. Talk a little faster. Become intense. Gesticulate. Get excited!

Do these two suggestions for building enthusiasm *really* work in everyday life?

Let's let Bob Allan answer this question. Bob worked for a chain store organization in a large city. This chain owned stores in both small towns and cities and was always on the lookout for alert, resourceful young men for management jobs in the small towns.

One day the general manager sent for Bob and offered him the job of managing a store in a small town quite some distance from his home city. The new job would offer him a substantial increase in salary, plus a bonus arrangement for increasing sales. Also better working conditions, an opportunity to be his own boss, and chances for advancement to a larger store.

On the negative side, it would mean leaving the city where he had all his friends and connections. His wife, their relatives, and others strongly advised him not to accept it, urged him not to bury himself in a small town far from his familiar surroundings and the many advantages of the big city.

But Bob, after carefully weighing the advantages and disadvantages, decided to accept the new job. He persuaded his wife it was the thing to do, and he went one step further. He decided that if the job was worth accepting, it was worth accepting with enthusiasm.

When Bob moved, he kept uppermost in his mind the many advantages of the new job and of his new way of living. He deliberately erased from his mind all thoughts of his former life in the city. Occasionally when he caught himself thinking about "the good old days," he pushed the thoughts to one side.

Bob made it a point on every occasion to let his new neighbors know just how excited he was about living in their town. His enthusiasm was so contagious that he resold several old-timers on their own town. Everybody liked him and sought him out. He attracted customers into his store, and his business prospered. He was invited to join the local clubs and organizations, and he became a leader in the civic and social life of the community. Because of his habit of being enthusiastic, Bob is well on his way to greater achievements.

The principal trait employers look for in job seekers is enthusiasm. The value of enthusiasm was confirmed by a recent survey conducted for Minnegasco, Inc., a business firm in Minneapolis, in which both job hunters and employers were interviewed. The survey found that, interestingly enough, although job seekers ranked their work-related experience as most important, only 3 percent of employers agreed. The employers rated enthusiasm as the number-one characteristic, and the most important quality they looked for in a job applicant.

If you want to see enthusiasm in action, watch a group of children on their way to the circus to see the elephants, the funny clowns, and the man on the flying trapeze. They can already taste the popcorn and smell the sawdust. Their eyes sparkle; their voices are shrill; their bodies are tense with excitement. Children are the greatest of all enthusiasts because they are not ashamed to let others see their enthusiasm. When you want to act enthusiastic, just remember how you felt and acted when you were a child on the way to the circus.

Enthusiasm is always associated with youth. But all of us must stay young at heart and keep our enthusiasm.

Hanging on the wall behind General MacArthur's desk hung this message:

Youth is not a time of life—it is a state of mind. Nobody grows old merely by living a number of years. People grow old by deserting their ideals. Years wrinkle the skin, but to give up enthusiasm wrinkles the soul.

Worry, doubt, self-distrust, fear and despair—these are the long, long years that bow the head and turn the growing spirit back to dust.

Whether you are seventy or sixteen, there is in the heart of every human being the love of wonder— the sweet amazement at the stars and the starlike things and thoughts—unfailing childlike appetite for what is coming next—and the joy and game of life.

You are as young as your faith and as old as your

doubt, as young as your self-confidence and as old as your fear, as young as your hope and as old as your despair.

THE BOTTOM LINE

1. All of us are born with some capacity for enthusiasm. Those who are determined to succeed nurture it as a dependable vehicle that will transport them to the top.

2. Sell yourself on the worth of your work and your personal ability. That new confidence must then be projected. The resulting enthusiasm you display will sell *you* to others.

3. Management looks at the amount of enthusiasm you display to determine your value as an employee. Honest enthusiasm is the chief indicator of your interest in the work and your ability to do it.

4. Only those determined to become old before their time have reason to stifle their enthusiasm. If "all the world loves a lover," the least likely candidate for early retirement is the person who lets the world know he *loves* his work.

5. Achievers learn early in the game to use enthusiasm as an aid to winning success.

8

SELECT A GOAL
—AND GO FOR IT!

*It isn't how smart you are or how much money you
have. It's how persistent you are. Your venture has
to outweigh everything else in your life. There can't
be two goals: if your goal is to make your business a
success, your goal can't be to own a Ferrari.*

—PHIL AKIN,
twenty-three, millionaire entrepreneur.

Webster's New Collegiate Dictionary defines the word
goal as "The end toward which effort is directed." Obviously, anyone about to expend any effort should have
some goal in mind before he begins. Yet, selecting a goal
and going about the business of attaining it is a problem
that has troubled mankind down through the ages. The
individual with the best chance of reaching his goal is
the person who has developed another special character
trait that might be called *singleness of purpose.*

Without a specific destination in mind we become

like the young fellow who went up to the ticket window
in a Chicago railroad station and said, "Give me a ticket
to Springfield." The clerk then asked him, "Springfield,
Illinois; Springfield, Massachusetts; Springfield, Missouri? Which do you want? There's a Springfield in
every one of the lower forty-eight states, young man!
What's your choice?"

After a few seconds, the hesitant traveler replied,
"I'll take the cheapest."

This tongue-in-cheek example may be a bit extreme, but the hard truth is that too many select their
lifework in a manner that is similarly as thoughtless.
Snap-judgment careerists are the ones who wake up
during their forties feeling disappointed. They spend
most of their remaining prime years counting the days
until their retirement.

The true achievers, in every walk of life, made their
marks only after establishing specific goals for themselves. Once they determined exactly what they wanted
to accomplish, they went for it! Each of them developed
a singleness of purpose that made failure nearly impossible. None of them managed to escape disappointments
or setbacks along the way, but their refusal to admit defeat made them winners in the long run.

As was stressed in Chapter 3, on finding the right
work, you have already hurdled your biggest single ob-
stacle to success when you find a job that is both challenging and enjoyable. In addition to developing your
mind and providing you with specific skills that will
qualify you for a wide range of occupations, a college
education also gives you time to decide on a career that
suits your aptitudes and needs. Those intent on climbing
aboard the winner's bandwagon set specific goals for

themselves even before they land their first jobs. In days past, making a decent living was goal enough for the disadvantaged. Charlie O'Connell, an exuberant Irish-American from Brooklyn, loved to make light of the way he began his long and successful career in business.

Charlie reached his sixteenth birthday shortly after the turn of the century, and he depended on the strong matriarch of the O'Connell family to guide him into his first paying job. Mrs. O'Connell studied the help wanted ads in the *Brooklyn Eagle* and deliberately circled three, all calling for a bright young office boy. Her reason for selecting the three had more to do with her motherly instincts than some Godgiven talent for employment counseling. His mother was concerned about her son's safety, so she settled for companies located very close to the first subway stop in Manhattan where young Charlie wanted to work.

With his mother accompanying him, Charlie had a successful interview at his first call, the company closest to the subway stop. The position paid the princely sum of five dollars per week, and Mrs. O'Connell was especially pleased with her son's one "fringe benefit": a daily free lunch. That very fanciful reason for taking a job worked well for Charlie O'Connell. He spent his entire career with the same company and was earning considerably more than five dollars weekly by retirement. At the ceremonial dinner in his honor, he brought the house down with the closing line of his retirement speech: "I have often wondered what would have happened if my mother and I had called that morning on the *second* company on our list!"

Although the remark was made in jest, everyone in the banquet room had reason to ponder that question

along with Charlie. His reasons for settling on his lifetime career were as offbeat as they came, but O'Connell's single-mindedness made it work splendidly for
him. Once on the job, even at his tender years, he found
that he liked everything about it—the excitement of
being a part of a growing organization, his bosses and
fellow employees, and the sense of accomplishment at
the end of each day. He remained an office boy for a
very brief time, and his ability and attitude won him
many promotions. Before long, he was forced to consider tempting offers from rival firms, but Charlie had
already set goals for himself, goals that became ever
more challenging as his experience grew. His ultimate
goal was to become an officer in the company before he
retired, and—fifty years, three wars, and five depres-
sions later—the traditional gold watch was presented to
Charles O'Connell, *vice-president.* It was no small accomplishment because his company had grown over
those fifty years into one of America's largest corporations.

O'Connell's story is heartwarming because he succeeded despite the heavy odds against him. There was
certainly an incredible element of luck involved in his
finding a small niche in a business he grew to love. A
strong case can also be made that anyone with his lack
of formal education would have little chance, in today's
supercompetitive job market, to achieve the same kind
of success.

But—and it's a very big *but*—the only pure element of *luck* in Charlie's story was his unorthodox
means of choosing a career. Once he accepted the five
bucks per week, he became a walking, talking, producing example of all the winning character traits we are

examining in this book. He began immediately to set goals for himself, small ones in the beginning, in keeping with his youth and inexperience. Once they were attained, he worked diligently to pull himself up to the next level he wanted to reach. He may have taken a job closest to the subway station, but he wasn't going to settle for a ride to the cheapest Springfield. Once he boarded the work train, he refused to be tempted by any of the stations along the way where the grass looked greener and more tempting.

The Sooner the Better

There are countless success stories, several in this book, of people who started careers in one area and then went on to great success in another. Obviously, they were forced to struggle longer because of their misguided original choices. For that reason finding the *right* work and striving for goals with a *singleness of purpose* are related but not synonymous topics. The goals you aim for must encompass both your career and your private life. They will enable you to answer the final question: "Just what have I accomplished?"

There's an old French proverb that says, "Be careful what you set your heart on, for you will *surely* get it!" Like a Gallic shrug, the proverb can have at least two meanings. On one level, it's an encouragement. On the other, it's a warning that you had better know what you want out of life or you'll live to regret it. Because setting one's life goals is such a universally perplexing problem, the more time you have to do so, the more likely you are to come up with the correct answer. Because you will have to utilize singleness of purpose to achieve those goals, carefully select and define them as soon as possible. How soon? That depends entirely on the individual.

Most of us are not fortunate enough to know from childhood just what we want to do with our lives. Acclaimed soprano Beverly Sills was a notable exception to that rule. Miss Sills knew she wanted to become an opera singer, "like Lily Pons," even before she entered the first grade. She won an amateur singing contest at the age of three and was performing regularly as a professional singer and actress on network radio before she "retired" at the age of twelve to devote full time to her regular education. Even when she refused to surrender her goal to sing in the opera, and she continued voice studies with a distinguished vocal coach and gave special concentration to her daily French and Italian lessons that would prepare her for future roles.

By the time she was fifteen, Beverly Sills had mastered fifteen operatic roles. She had spent almost her entire young life preparing herself for the dream she had first envisioned when she was a toddler. She made her professional opera debut as Frasquita in Bizet's *Carmen* with the Philadelphia Civic Opera in February 1947, but she considered that only a beginner's step en route to her ultimate goal. She had long since set her sights high: she wanted to be a star of the New York City Opera. Her father's death forced her to seek employment wherever she could find it—usually in one-night stands in cross-country tours—but even eight years of struggle and numerous unsuccessful auditions with City Opera failed to undermine her determination.

In the end, her singleness of purpose paid off and,

on October 29, 1955, she made her triumphant debut as Rosalinde in Johann Strauss's *Die Fledermaus*. The critics raved, as if she had sprung full-blown out of nowhere. True to her character, Beverly made new and more challenging goals, which she reached and surpassed. She became an internationally celebrated coloratura soprano, thrilling audiences in opera houses and concert halls all over the world. When she retired from active performing, her beloved New York City Opera company refused to allow the many skills that had made her an outstanding achiever go to waste. She was named to head the entire operation of the opera company that had nurtured her singing talent. In this role she became one of the few women ever to enter opera's top administrative ranks.

Set Realistic Goals

Naturally, it would be the height of folly for a tone-deaf woman with a voice like Francis the talking mule to set her sights on following in the footsteps of Beverly Sills. Likewise, it should be apparent that there are more openings for junior executives, managers, department heads, and other salaried workers than there are for chairmen of the board or chief executive officers. Setting goals that are virtually unattainable can lead to frustration and despair.

Lionel Barrymore, a great star of stage and screen for many decades, had his own view on the subject. "I believe," he once said, "that if a man sets an attainable goal for himself and works to attain it, . . . he will have for this reason a full, busy and a happy life." That simple philosophy seems almost too passive when compared to the credo of another Hollywood legend. Cecil B. De Mille, pioneer producer of some of the most successful pictures in film history, said: "Most of us serve our ambitions by fits and starts. The person who makes a success of living is the one who sees his goal steadily and aims for it unswervingly." However, both men make common points: goals must be set, and the vigorous pursuit of those goals will bring happiness and success.

You may tell yourself that it is impractical to set your sights on a goal that only a select few in the history of mankind have been able to reach. Fair enough: that proves you have your feet on the ground. But there is no law that says you cannot keep that impossible dream in the back of your mind while you use every resource at your command to come as close to it as your best efforts can take you. Like a baseball team that aspires to winning the World Series, you must win one game at a time. If you manage to get into the World Series and fail to reach the ultimate goal, remember that winning the National or American League Championship is still a great achievement.

Above all, do not build a fence around your potential! Too many people are defeated before they start by *self-imposed* limits on what they think they can achieve. They prove that humans are susceptible to the psychological failings of goldfish. Psychologists have tested the conditioning of goldfish by placing them in a tank of water that had an invisible glass partition at one end separating the fish from a tempting supply of their favorite food. The fish saw the food and, for twenty days, kept smashing at the glass barrier trying to get at it. Completely frustrated by their unsuccessful efforts, they finally gave up. When the psychologist eventually removed the partition, the fish did not even try to get at the now-available food. They had been conditioned never to try.

All of us, for one reason or another, carry some kind of "invisible glass partition" with us throughout our youth. Many of us continue to struggle with it for the rest of our lives. Whatever form it takes, it can be a lethal handicap to the singleness of purpose necessary to reach our greatest goals. The history of running provides a concrete example. It was always believed that it was impossible for any human being to run a mile in fewer than four minutes. Some came close to that mark, but no one ever cracked it. Sports writers wrote of "the four-minute barrier."

There was one man in the world, an obscure English miler named Roger Bannister, who did not buy the impossibility theory. He refused to acknowledge any invisible barrier, and, on May 6, 1954, Bannister ran his way into the history books by becoming the first human to break the 4-minute barrier. His time was 3 minutes, 59.4 seconds. Then what happened? In the next two years no fewer than twelve men also accomplished "the impossible" and broke the 4-minute barrier, many of them bettering Bannister's record. Later, Irishman Eamonn Coughlin held the indoor mile record with the astonishing mark of 3 minutes, 49.78 seconds—10 seconds faster than Bannister's pioneering time. The point is, every runner who runs the mile in fewer than 4 minutes owes a debt of gratitude to Roger Bannister because he was the first to prove that the impossible barrier didn't exist.

It is never too late to learn or to apply yourself to

work that you enjoy, but it is always best to find the area in which you can best achieve as soon as you possibly can. Putting off the effort necessary to reach a lofty but attainable goal only makes your task more difficult. Some believe it's best to wait until they have tasted life from every angle before they "settle down" into a career. They may be putting themselves in the position where they'll have to settle for a ticket to the cheapest Springfield. Little is gained and much can be squandered in the long search for the perfect career.

Someone with great wisdom once said that a goal that is not written down on paper is just an idle dream and nothing more. Even if you choose not to take pen and paper in hand, make certain you print your goals on the computer of your *mind.* Once you know where you want to go, you can start developing that most important of mind-sets, *singleness of purpose.* Everyone who makes the world take notice has it—whether he or she started very early or very late in life. Two immortals in the arts illustrate the point.

Wolfgang Amadeus Mozart showed astonishing musical ability at an age when most children are learning their "do-re-mis" and toured the capitals of Europe as a child prodigy. He actually published violin sonatas in Paris and London before the age of ten. In spite of his impoverished childhood, he lived for his music and went on to fulfill his ambition to become one of the great musical composers of all time. His music lives and so does the story of his quest, thanks to its revelation in a medium he might never have dreamed about, the modern motion picture.

At the other end of the achiever's age scale is a woman the world remembers as Grandma Moses. Born into an era when women were instructed that their place was in the home, Mrs. Moses's career was her home and family until very late in her life. Yet, we remember her as a painter although she never touched an artist's brush until she reached an age when other painters have retired or died. Her stated goal as a primitive painter was simple: she wanted to reproduce the scenes she remembered from her childhood. She never stopped painting until her death at the age of one hundred. Two of her paintings of snow scenes in rural upstate New York, generally recognized as among her best, were started and finished after her one hundredth birthday. Her paintings continue to be displayed in major art museums across the country, and they have steadily risen in monetary value.

These two extraordinary masters of their chosen way of life displayed admirable singleness of purpose although they were of different sexes, nationalities, and fields of endeavor. One started at a very young age and the other began a new career very late in life. Neither ever deviated from his or her chosen course.

We can profit from their example. Choose *your* course, set your standards high, and let nothing and no one sway you from your goal.

THE BOTTOM LINE

1. Choose your field of endeavor carefully, but enter it with a will as soon as you are certain you have the proper education, aptitude, and motivation.

2. Once you have entered the work force, or even

before, write down exactly what you expect to achieve in your career. Set goals that are attainable.

3. Do not impose automatic limits on your potential. If you set goals that are too easily reached, you will lose sight of what you *can* do. If necessary, divide your goals into two categories: immediate and ultimate.

4. Once you have ascertained your goals, let nothing steer you off your course. Develop singleness of purpose, and you will find that discouragement and setbacks are only temporary. You *will* reach your goal!

9

THINKING:
THE INEXPENSIVE
ENERGY SAVER

Concentration is my motto—first honesty, then industry, then concentration.

—ANDREW CARNEGIE

All of us, provided with even a normal proportion of gray matter, have the wonderful ability to think. Yet, faced with the daily activity of hurdling barriers, we become so bogged down that we give too little thought to removing them. We spend so much of our valuable time reacting to events that we have little time left in which to initiate action.

Americans, possibly more than any other people on earth, are weaned from birth to become "men of action." That's all to the good, as the stories of accom-

plishment by American men and women have proved.
However, we can sometimes learn valuable lessons from
others, including our enemies.

The story goes that the victorious Allied armies
learned an especially intriguing bit of information about
their defeated German enemies when they moved into a
German army headquarters at the end of World War II.

In going through the personnel files in the occupied
headquarters, it is said, the Allies found the individual
records of every commissioned officer in the German
Army. Each officer's file listed the battles in which he
had fought and the details of his individual participation. That was interesting enough, but the Americans
and British were baffled and fascinated by some mysterious marks they found in each file. It was eventually determined that the marks were something of a shorthand
code, describing each officer. Each record carried one of
these four classifications: S & L, B & I, S & I, and B & L.

The beginning of the mystery was solved with the
discovery that *B* stood for brilliant, *S* for stupid, *I* for industrious, and *L* for lazy. Of course, that still didn't explain the riddle of why some of the Germans were
classified B & L—brilliant and lazy—or S & I—stupid
and industrious. It seemed that these combinations and
others were almost contradictory. The Allied Intelligence people then matched these terse classifications
against the actual wartime records of the German officers.

As expected, the complete records showed that the
men classified brilliant and industrious made good field
officers. The stupid and lazy made the worst officers.
Ironically, the stupid and *industrious* proved to be complete disasters, disproving the maxim that hard work

alone will make you successful. These were the men who had little idea what they were doing but worked twenty-four hours a day to bring it about.

Which lettered group worked out the best? The B & L! To everyone's suprise, those officers classified brilliant and *lazy* proved to be the most effective group of officers in the German Army. These men were the successful planners, the innovators, the men who manned the so-called think tanks—the real brains of the army. The German military machine labeled them lazy because they did not give the appearance of being men of action. They were often seen sitting silently for hours, or walking absentmindedly through the woods, lost in thought.

Their action took a different form, a form that actually kept the Nazis in the war longer than would have been possible without them. Their "brilliant laziness" enabled them to create the rockets and other new forms of weaponry that made the Germans so difficult to defeat. They were a part of the High Command—the achievers. They were the relatively small body of men in the High Command who took the time, even during the period of greatest stress during the final days of the war, to think about how to carry on despite the odds against them. Fortunately, they were unable to prevail; otherwise Germany might have won the war.

What is to be learned from the German experience? Neither pure brilliance nor fanatical dedication is really enough to carry you all the way to the top. *Action,* for the sake of action alone, can often do more harm than good. The individual who spends some time in serious thinking will come up with an easier and better way to do the things he is trying to accomplish.

Take Time to Think

Far too many executives and other leaders never seem to find the time to step back from the daily grind and give serious thought to new and better ways to do their jobs. If they can't find time for this all-important activity, then they must *make* time.

What keeps them from thinking? Mostly other people! It's impossible to do any constructive thinking about your long-range problems when you're talking or listening to someone else. And yet this is what most of us do all day long. We have to keep processing the work that comes over our desks—reading and answering more and more correspondence; taking telephone calls; interviewing employees and customers; attending committee meetings, industry affairs, get-togethers at our service clubs and the chamber of commerce; and on and on. The days aren't long enough, and everything fights for our attention—*except creative thinking.*

The basic demands of our jobs cannot be ignored, but a typical logjam like this demands a rearrangement of our priorities. Serious, productive thinking must be given the highest importance. It must assume a role on the same level as your responsibilities to your family and your personal health and physical fitness. The answer is to set aside a definite time and a specific place to do your deep thinking. This task will not be an easy one. If it were, the world would be crowded with creative thinkers and you know it isn't. But it is a job that must be done, on company time or on your own.

The great Oliver Wendell Holmes, U.S. Supreme Court justice and author of *The Common Law*, spoke and wrote much about the opportunities for solitary thinking while walking. In praise of this activity he said: "In walking, the will and the muscles are so accustomed to working together, and perform their task with so little expenditure of force, that the intellect is left comparatively free."

Another eminent walker-thinker is one of America's favorite living authors, James Michener. Thinking is such an integral part of writing that the creator of *Hawaii, Chesapeake, Texas,* and a number of other bestsellers swears by it. He claims, in fact, "When my writing goes poorly, it is always because I have not walked enough. For it is on these uneventful and repetitious walks that I do my best thinking."

Finding Your Private Space

You may have your own magnificently appointed office that is supposed to be your private space. But is it? Too often it simply becomes the place where everyone knows you can be reached. It is far more important to find some area where you can enjoy the ultimate and most necessary solitude, the privacy of your innermost thoughts. Holmes, Michener, and a multitude of others—writers, scientists, inventors, researchers, business planners—have found that walking alone provides a perfect time and place for deep thinking and planning. Their system may also work well for you.

It's not necessary to emulate Thoreau and seek the magnificent isolation of Walden Pond. The scene that unfolds around you is unimportant. What matters is the scene that is created *behind* your eyes. Walking can give you an opportunity for solitude, even if it's done during the middle of rush hour on crowded Manhattan Island. Many busy men and women make a habit of getting up a half hour earlier in the morning in order to walk to work. This gives them a special time at the start of each working day when they can give their undivided attention, without interruption, to the problems they're certain to face before evening.

That solution to finding time to think, because walking is such a good form of exercise, reminds us of Abe Lincoln's sage advice—"He who cuts his own firewood is warmed twice." He who walks to work is twice blessed—he finds time to think and becomes the healthier for it.

Are you a "day" or a "night" person? Science has proved that people do function better at different times of the day. Many men and women find that they are at their brightest in the early morning hours, refreshed by their night's sleep, their minds free of extraneous thoughts. Morning can be a profitable time for them to think ahead—and come up with some workable solutions to their work problems.

For others, the best time of the day is the *twenty minutes* they allow themselves each morning between waking up and actually getting out of bed. If you keep a pad and a pencil on your bedside stand, you will be able to record your best thoughts before they are lost. Your mind will be rested, all will be quiet, and you will be able to concentrate.

There are still others who, like the desert cactus *Cereus*, bloom only at night. Many so-called night people really do their most creative thinking at night. For some, the later the hour the better it suits them. A Los

Angeles oil executive furnished a small basement of his suburban home. Here, late at night when the other family members had gone to bed, he was really able to concentrate. It was too late for distracting telephone calls or other interruptions, and he considered it his most rewarding time of day.

The point is, if you are willing to work harder to become a true achiever, you must also be prepared to sacrifice some of your work or leisure time to think and plan. Ideally, you will be able to clear some office time each day like the Atlanta banker who instructs his secretary to transfer no telephone calls or admit no callers for the first thirty minutes after he begins his day. He allows very few exceptions to that rule, and his associates have come to accept the fact that he won't be "in" to anyone early in his workday. But, if you are unable to clear free thinking time at the office, it is essential that you find it elsewhere, even on your own time.

If you are one of the countless millions who have become disciplined adherents of physical fitness, you have a perfect opportunity to combine two worthwhile habits. There certainly will be no one to distract you if you are a long-distance runner or swimmer. In fact, some heavy thinking about the knottiest problems in your career will actually take your mind off your aching lungs and muscles and make these activities less monotonous.

It's clear that it would be unhealthy to devote every waking moment to thinking about your problems at work. But inner problem solving on your own time will inevitably make your workday less stressful. Most of us like to consider the weekends inviolate—*our time*—designed to afford us some beneficial amnesia about the workplace. True enough, but the weekends can also afford us some excellent free time, in a relaxed atmosphere, when we can think about the problems of the past week and those bound to arise in the upcoming five days. It would be inspiring to be able to list all the inventions that have been conceived, all the sales promotions dreamed up, all the great book ideas "accidentally" discovered by men and women who were far away from their actual offices and desks.

The hackneyed expression "the thinking man" did not come into the language by chance. Any successful individual must also be a *thinking* person—it comes with the territory. Donald Regan, at this writing, is one of the most powerful and busiest men in our nation's capital. He has become closer to President Reagan than anyone else in the government. His life story reads like the realization of the American Dream.

Regan grew up in a blue-collar neighborhood of Cambridge, Massachusetts. His father was a railroad security guard, and the young Irish-American and his family were determined that he would do better when he reached manhood. By working nights and Saturdays and Sundays, Donald Regan managed to graduate from Harvard. After World War II he took a job as a trainee at Merrill Lynch, one of the most important brokerage houses on Wall Street. He and his young family were transferred to new locations a dozen times during his early years with the company, but with each transfer came a promotion. At the age of forty-nine he became president of Merrill Lynch.

In the next ten years, Regan proved to be a daring leader who was able to institute many changes and new programs. Under his management, the company's business doubled and, by his sixtieth birthday, Donald Regan's personal wealth was more than $30 million. This kind of progressive leadership ability prompted a surprise telephone call from President-elect Ronald Reagan and the offer of the post of secretary of the Treasury in the new cabinet. Regan's four years as head man at the Treasury Department impressed the president so much that he wanted the self-made millionaire to take an even more active role in the next administration. Regan switched jobs with James Baker and became White House chief of staff, the literal "right-hand man" of the chief executive.

In his role as the second most powerful man in the administration, Regan must be on constant call, ready to handle every possible type of emergency. Can a man in this position—a man whose first duty is to relieve the pressure from another—find time for his own serious thinking? His associates report that he works an *eleven-hour day*. He is productively busy from early morning until midafternoon. It is then that he has *created his own time for creative thinking*. Except for extreme emergency, this time is his special uninterrupted period when he can organize his own thoughts and plans with the same efficiency with which he manages the president's schedule.

The achievers are the creative thinkers of the world—the innovators, the discoverers, the problem solvers. You cannot aspire to creative thinking until you have made a habit of actually analyzing the tasks assigned to you. Precipitous action without proper thought and evaluation can develop the destructive power of a pebble rolling down a loose-shale mountainside. Reserve a time, in or out of the office, that will be yours without interruption or distraction. It is the world's most inexpensive energy saver.

THE BOTTOM LINE

1. Schedule each day in a way that you can have some time, however brief, when you can have an uninterrupted period of concentrated thinking.

2. *Thinking* is ultimately the most important part of your work. It should not necessarily be restricted to regular office hours.

3. Are you a day or night person? If you find it impossible to clear time at the office, learn the time of day when your mind is most alert and creative and use it to ponder your problems and make your plans. Preserve your best ideas in a notepad.

4. Walking, jogging, swimming, and other physical fitness activities lend themselves nicely to thinking. Learn to "kill two birds with one stone."

10

WORDS ARE WORTH MONEY

Words have a magical power. They can bring either the greatest happiness or deepest despair; can transfer knowledge from teacher to student; words enable the orator to sway his audience and dictate its decision. Words are capable of arousing the strongest emotions and prompting all men's actions.
—SIGMUND FREUD

Words are the tools of thinking and, as Freud points out, the tools of communication with others. No good carpenter or automobile mechanic would even dream of approaching a house or car without the essential tools that lighten his labor and make it possible for him to complete his work. Yet, many of us in careers that stress mental rather than physical labor come to our jobs with a grossly inadequate supply of *our* most important tools: *words.* It is often forgotten that words are the tools of *thinking!* The size of a person's vocabulary influences his ability to think and either expands or limits his capacity to communicate with others.

It is most thwarting when we cannot say exactly what we mean because we don't know the precise word or words. Without words we cannot express our thoughts verbally or on paper.

The ability to communicate adds a zest to our lives. It is fun, it is satisfying, it makes us feel good about ourselves. It builds our self confidence and opens many doors to opportunities in business and friendships. It does all this for us providing that we have the means to express ourselves. What are these means: words and more words.

If you doubt this, just imagine that you have moved to France. You have very little command or knowledge of the French language, except a familiarity with the few French words and phrases that you recall from your two years of study in high school. Your ability to communicate with others is limited to the few words you have already learned. You manage to make your needs known to porters, cabdrivers, waiters, but you can only find your lost luggage through the concierge who speaks English, understands your problem, and locates it for you through the airline.

This is only one frustrating experience; the most irritating is your lack of French vocabulary so you cannot exchange ideas about anything with anyone with the same background as you.

This mental voyage has not been a pleasure. You now put yourself back in the United States. Here you have a much larger vocabulary in English. After all it is your native tongue. However, you honestly admit that you frequently find yourself at a loss for just the words you want to express your thoughts. You realize it is difficult or even impossible to explain your ideas to another because you lack the proper words.

When you start adding words to your vocabulary, you are increasing your opportunities to get ahead, to achieve your goals in life, much more than you may believe.

Dr. Johnson O'Connor, a scientific research expert, wrote in the *Atlantic* on this subject. "An extensive knowledge of the exact meanings of English words accompanies outstanding success in this country more than any other characteristics which the Human Engineering Laboratories have been able to isolate and measure."

Dr. O'Connor's evaluation of the advantages of a good vocabulary was based on proven fact. The Human Engineering Laboratories conducted wide research into the matter, using a list of 150 test words to measure the extent of an individual's vocabulary. The selected word, printed in italics, was part of a short phrase presented to the person being tested. The individual was then asked to select one of five given synonyms nearest in meaning to the italicized word. The test words, all found in general reading material, were selected by Alexander Ingles of the Graduate School of Education at Harvard University. Technical words were deliberately omitted because the test was designed to measure recognizable words that might be used in everyday conversation. A wide range of groups and individuals were tested.

Three hundred high school freshmen averaged 75 errors on the 150-word test. Seven hundred and fifty college freshmen averaged 42 errors. One thousand college graduates, from a wide spectrum of institutions, averaged 27 errors. One of the highest-scoring groups tested, not surprisingly, was a large sampling of college professors. The professional academicians averaged only 8 errors in the 150-word test. For all the individuals tested, the scores ranged from one person who knew fewer than 50 of the 150 words, to the one person in a thousand who achieved a pefect score.

The researchers at the Human Engineering Laboratories compiled the standings of those who generally scored highest on the vocabulary test according to occupation. Top business executives averaged only seven errors! They actually exhibited a better vocabulary than college professors. These individuals were top-echelon executives who, for five years or longer had held the position of chairman or president of a business organization.

The business leaders selected for testing were chosen from companies that were hugely successful and from others that had done less well, although the latter were fewer in number. They included men with dynamic, forceful personalities and others who did their work quietly as figureheads. However, the testing had the great advantage, as will be seen later, of excluding all personal judgment from the process of selection.

It is generally agreed that it is extremely difficult, if not impossible, to define success accurately and scientifically. Nevertheless, it seemed to the scientists of the Human Engineering Laboratories that a large vocabulary is a common characteristic in almost all successful individuals, regardless of their particular occupation.

For example, the laboratories also discovered that successful members of the legal and medical professions also scored unusually high.

Success, like beauty, may often be in the eye of the beholder. Even the dictionary gives several definitions for *success,* one of which is "A high degree of worldly prosperity." That definition correlates closely with the findings of the Human Engineering Laboratories. Their testing proved that the measured English vocabulary of a business executive had a direct influence on the salary he earned. In other words, the larger the vocabulary, the larger the paycheck. There were a few exceptions to the rule, but the research gave a strong indication that words really are worth money!

There was one very noticeable exception to the belief that higher education also generates a larger vocabulary. One executive interviewed was reluctant to take part in the testing at the beginning. He had come from a family that could not afford the cost of education, and his formal schooling had ended at the age of fourteen. he was well spoken and had scored high on the aptitude tests, but he was certain that a good vocabulary was a product of higher education. He had no desire to cause himself undue embarrassment. After much persuasion, he agreed to take part in the experiment and came through with colors flying—making only 2 errors! Imagine his pleasure when he was told that the average college graduate produced 27 incorrect answers.

All the tests were given and the results recorded at Stevens Institute of Technology in Hoboken, New Jersey. Special note was made of the occupation of each person tested. That made it easier, for example, for the researchers to list the vocabulary scores of 100 business executives right alongside those of 100 randomly selected college graduates. In that direct comparison, only 9 percent of the college graduates, in a variety of fields, scored as high as the achievers in commerce.

It seems clear that the men and women who have risen to be top executives and leaders in business and the professions developed very early in their careers an awareness of the power of words. These individuals have mastered the ability to use the exact words needed to convey their opinions and thoughts. It is obvious that anyone communicating with the public, with clients, with associates, with subordinates in the course of the day did not accumulate a large vocabulary because of what he or she learned on the job. Skills in word usage are irreplaceable tools that helped each and every one to reach the summit in his business and profession.

Don't Be Typecast by Your Speech

To this day, it's nearly impossible for a British native to disguise the *class* into which he or she was born. The manner in which the individual speaks the English language is a dead giveaway to other Britishers. The great Irish playwright George Bernard Shaw, a longtime resident of Britain, wrote one of his most successful plays on this subject. The Americans Alan Jay Lerner and Frederick Loewe later transformed it into a smash musical for stage and film under a new title, *My Fair Lady*.

In his original *Pygmalion*, as in the musical, Shaw's

premise was that a dedicated speech expert could pass off an uneducated Cockney flower seller to London society as a well-bred lady simply by upgrading her manner of speech. Shaw's Henry Higgins was mostly concerned with correcting Eliza Doolittle's accent before she made her social debut, but he also supplied her with an adequate vocabulary that would enable her to conduct herself properly. The unexpected problems Higgins and Eliza encountered along the way have made their story an international classic.

In America as nowhere else in this world the opportunity to rise from humble beginnings to the highest office in the land, that of the Presidency, has been proved, Abraham Lincoln being the best-known example to all. The class system does not play an important part in our way of life. It didn't in "honest Abe's" day; it doesn't now. However, in communicating with others today one must speak well. Regional accents are less prevalent because of television and movies. We are becoming a more homogenized society. The person who has taken time to acquire an extensive vocabulary, and who knows how to use it properly and flawlessly, is instantly recognized as someone who takes pride in his language and his ability to speak well.

More than any single attribute, the familiar and unaffected use of a vast vocabulary is an immediate indication of your intelligence and your learning. Ironically, especially among those with higher education, the vocabulary usually stops growing when the average person reaches the age of twenty-five. The principal reason for this is the excuse that we're too *busy* to concern ourselves with learning new words. Yet, research has

proved that our chances for success increase in proportion to the strength of our vocabularies.

How to Expand Your Vocabulary

Visit the office of any professional writer worth reading
and you are certain to see at least two books within easy
reach of his work surface: a good *dictionary* and a copy
of *Roget's Thesaurus.* These dedicated, solitary workers
know that their ultimate success or failure depends entirely on the strength and effectiveness of the words they
put on paper with pen, pencil, typewriter, or word processor. To a smaller extent, *so does yours!*

If you are determined to be a leader, you must
command an effective vocabulary to inspire maximum
production from those who follow you. In a sense, your
need for word power is even more vital than the
writer's, because he will usually communicate to large
groups only on paper whereas your skills must be honed
for both written and *spoken* effectiveness. For this reason, make certain that you have good dictionaries and
thesauruses in both your home and office. Make a habit
of referring to them as often as possible. Because little
can be as boring as constant repetition, the thesaurus
will be especially helpful. Among its more than 240,000
English words, broken down into nouns, verbs, adverbs,
and adjectives, it provides countless synonyms that will
allow you considerable verbal variety.

Do not simply buy these books, place them on a
shelf, and consider your work done. Use them! Nothing
equals *reading* as a method of expanding your vocabulary. Read the classics of American and English litera-

ture and books on any other subjects that interest you. Be aware of the new words you come across and look them up if you are not certain of their meaning. Good periodicals such as *Time* and *Newsweek* can also be profitable leisure-time companions, simultaneously helping to increase your knowledge of current events and your word power. The same can be said of appropriate trade papers and magazines. Always look up words that seem unfamiliar. Many people have doubled and tripled their vocabulary in less than a year by using this simple method.

Many of us, snowed under with constant career pressure, dread the idea of picking up a weighty volume with the idea of either entertaining ourselves or improving our minds. We feel we left all of that sort of thing behind with college. But reading is actually the simplest and most natural way of increasing your knowledge of words. Our vocabulary growth slows to a trickle past the age of twenty-five because we have what the experts call an active and a passive recall of words. Your *active vocabulary* contains the words you use in everyday conversation; your *passive vocabulary* contains words whose meanings you know but rarely, if ever, use in normal conversation. Begin using these half-forgotten words so they become part of your active vocabulary. Only the vocabulary you use can contribute to your effectiveness as an achiever.

In perfecting any area in the art of self-management, it is first necessary to sit down and take a good look at yourself. Does your vocabulary measure up to the goals you have set for yourself? Are you able to explain yourself or your ideas in easy, concise terms that leave no doubt about your position? Is your normal conversation studded with a surplus of "uhs" and "you knows"? Do you find yourself in awe of the confident manner in which a friend or associate speaks? If you have any doubt at all about the way you speak or write when you attempt to project your ideas, *it's time you started a serious personal program of vocabulary improvement!*

If you consider your vocabulary sadly inadequate and a handicap to your progress, investigate the possibility of enrolling in a course of word building at a night class in your local college. It's possible to gain a similar advantage by signing up for a home-study course in the extension division of your state university. And if you cannot budget your free time for these options, you can get fine results from a painless do-it-yourself program. There are many excellent books that demonstrate proven methods of improving anyone's vocabulary. One you might consider is *Thirty Days to a More Powerful Vocabulary* by Wilfred Funk and Norman Lewis (1970).

By all means, make good use of your dictionary and thesaurus. They will constantly remind you of the advantage in utilizing words that have slipped into your passive vocabulary. Set specific goals for yourself, use effective new words in your daily conversation, and the results will be rewarding. The way others *hear* you is as important as the way they *see* you. Investing the necessary time to perfect your facility with words will pay high dividends.

There are some who may hold the negative belief that using "five-dollar words" will eliminate them from automatic membership in that all-American club, "One of the Boys." Becoming a leader is not at all synonymous with losing the common touch. A good vocabulary, in this society, should not be an indication of snobbery. Words are simply the tools of thinking. Sprinkling your conversation with needlessly obscure words, which only a lexicographer might know, will not get the job done. Your listener will do more thinking about the unfamiliarity of the words than the thoughts they are meant to reveal.

Two of Britain's most famous sons had specific thoughts on the use of words, and both were eminently well qualified to speak on the matter. Dr. Samuel Johnson, the early lexicographer who helped to standardize and stabilize the English language, issued a simple warning: "Don't accustom yourself to use big words for little matters." Winston Churchill added, "A vocabulary of truth and simplicity will be of service throughout your life."

Mastering the language that enables you to communicate with others will serve you in every walk of life, and it will put you a quantum leap closer to becoming the achiever you intend to be.

THE BOTTOM LINE

1. The top leaders of business and industry rank high among those with word skills, and their salaries rise in direct proportion to their vocabularies.

2. If you have any degree of insecurity about your own vocabulary, start an immediate program to improve and expand it, beginning with the purchase of dictionaries and thesauruses for your home and office.

3. Set specific goals for yourself by learning and

using an agreed-upon number of new words each week. A good beginning: use your thesaurus to look up all the synonyms of a word you normally use in daily conversation and consciously substitute the alternatives.

4. If your education stressed technical training at the expense of language and literature, you can make up for that shortcoming by enrolling in night classes or extension courses.

5. In your reading and your work-related conversations, become *aware* of the way those you admire make good use of words. Dedicate yourself to reaching their level, or surpassing it.

11

GIVE THANKS FOR YOUR MEMORY

The secret of a good memory is attention, and attention to a subject depends upon our interest in it. We rarely forget that which has made a deep impression on our minds.

—TRYON EDWARDS

It has happened to all of us, and nothing is more frustrating than not being able to remember something that we know we should remember. How many times have you said, and heard others say, "It's on the tip of my tongue but I'll probably remember it when it is too late to matter." Sometimes this involves nothing more serious than the date of the opening of a new play, or the answer to a question in Trivial Pursuit, or the title of a novel you read recently. But at other times it can be of far greater importance: for instance being unable to recall the answer on a test, forgetting to send in a special report the boss requested, or forwarding important materials to a client. These are the times we become keenly aware of the shortcomings of our memory.

We are all born with essentially the same potential to build our memory but very few of us succeed in achieving anything near it. We should concentrate on reaching our full potential. It is a must—a personal task to help us toward success. As the football coaches each spring warn the newcomers, "If you want to make the team, you first have to master the fundamentals of the game—blocking, tackling, and handling the ball. These are the skills you must have before you can go out on the field and start making the big plays." This same advice applies to those preparing to get ahead in the professional or business world. Today there are techniques available to us—use them and teach them to your children and others. By putting forth a little bit of effort, you can make your memory one of your greatest assets.

Several years ago three ambitious junior executives, all working for the same New York company, wanted to improve their executive skills. They signed up, along with more than two hundred other ambitious ones, for an evening class at Columbia University in Executive Leadership.

At the first session the lecturer, like the football coach, told them, "If you want to be a top executive, you must first master the fundamentals of the job, the elementary skills, without which no executive can be successful."

At the top of his list were, among other skills, a large vocabulary, because no man can think beyond his store of words; the ability to write clearly and effectively in order to communicate; the ability to speak persuasively, to both groups and individuals; the ability to get along with people; and last but not least, a *memory* for names and places, past events and past decisions, so necessary to the effectiveness of any leader.

To many of the evening students who thought they were there to learn "the nuts and bolts" of running a business, this approach was a surprise. To others it was a disappointment. These students had only one reason for signing up for the course. They had hoped to learn enough in a few months to get a promotion and a salary increase. To them starting with fundamentals seemed retrogressive, and a great waste of time.

Our three junior executives, however, were sufficiently impressed with the logic of the approach to give it a try. Of all their basic skills, they felt they were weakest on *memory*.

Is Memory All That Important?

Dr. James Bender, who once taught a course at Columbia University on how to develop executive ability, says it is important:

> How much is it worth to a leader to double his powers of memory? Would greater ability to memorize names, figures, and facts increase his income in arithmetic or geometric proportion? That is to say, suppose you earn $4,000 a year. If you doubled your memory span, could you expect to increase your income to $28,000 or $56,000 annually?
>
> That depends upon the kind of work you do

and the present state of your "memorizer"; but fifteen top-flight high salaried executives were unanimous recently in saying, "As memorizing capacity doubles, earned income multiplies." The point is that a good memory is an excellent tool in almost any job. The greater your responsibilities, the more valuable a well-stocked memory becomes. Quite amazing, isn't it? Yet, when we stop to consider that a reliable memory saves time and builds good human relations—is it?

How You Can Improve Your Memory

Laird S. Cermak, Ph.D., professor and lecturer at Boston University, is involved in research on improving your memory. He tells us in his book *Improving Your Memory* that each of us actually has three different types of memory, all completely different. The three memory systems are *immediate memory*, *short-term memory*, and *long-term memory*.

Immediate memory is extremely limited. Attention is very important in determining what will or will not be responded to in immediate memory. This type of memory comes into play when you are listening to a conversation and someone says your name. You were discarding most of what you were hearing. The moment you heard your name it came into your immediate memory, and your reaction was to turn to the person who said your name to learn what else he had to say. If you had no immediate memory, you would forget that your name was spoken even before you responded to that call. It would be as if words went right through you. You could not hang on to them long enough to decide what they meant. It is immediate memory that enables us to discard information quickly to be ready for more important information.

Short-term memory. One of the most important items for all aspiring achievers to remember is *names.* People are pleased and sometimes even flattered when someone they meet for the second time remembers their name. It isn't always easy to recall names; most of us find it easier to remember faces. One of the techniques to help us is to pay more attention when we are introduced. Discard any notion that it is somewhat rude to look directly at another's face. Look directly at the person and repeat the name. The person to whom you are being introduced will respond to this increased attention by returning the glance and will begin to notice and listen to you. Good salespeople are very aware that a client will respond much more positively to a direct look than to an offhand glance. There are other learning devices to sharpen your ability to recall numbers, to develop ways to memorize multiple units, and to organize long-term memory.

Long-term memory involves three techniques: First is *mediation;* this procedure boils down to an attempt to verbalize everything in as significant a fashion as possible and then to store it in memory on a basis of a meaningful translation. To illustrate: an easy way to remember the names of the Great Lakes is to remember the word HOMES—Huron, Ontario, Michigan, Erie, Superior. Most of us learned this in elementary school and have never forgotten the Great Lakes' names.

The second technique of organization into long-term memory is *imagery,* translating information or an experience into a mental picture rather than into a meaningful word.

The final tool is *mnemonics,* which uses the first two, and once you have mastered this device, you will realize that it is one of the best procedures for the maintenance of information over extended period of time. Many people have learned to use mnemonic devices successfully. Just what is a mnemonic device?

It is a system that actually helps you recall all the things most people find difficult to remember—names, faces, places, numbers, dates of great importance. Dr. Bruno Furst, who taught memory-training courses for years in New York City, stressed the use of mnemonics. His courses took six weeks of night sessions and were well attended by business executives, lawyers, doctors, and young aspiring achievers. All who attended at any time attribute their recall ability to the interesting comprehensive way Dr. Furst taught the use of mnemonic devices. He wrote many books on the subject. However, he is not the only one of note in his field. Dr. Laird Cermak's book *Improving Your Memory* (some of which we have paraphrased in this chapter) will give you much more worthwhile information that we can only touch on in the confines of this book.

Lists. An easy system that requires neither monetary investment nor much time each day is to form the good habit of making a list.

Each morning, or the night before, whichever is more convenient, you make up your new list for the new day, carrying forward all the items you were not able to accomplish the previous day, plus the new ones added.

"Live by the list!" This daily list is probably the most valuable tool ever devised *for getting things done!*

No one else can make your list for you—not your secretary, not your executive assistant, not even your spouse—only you! Only you can operate this memory jogger, because you are the only one who knows all that you should do.

Many a man with brains, education, and a winning personality fails to get ahead because people have learned they can't count on him. "He's not dependable," they say. "He's not reliable; he's often late for or misses important appointments."

If you want to be known as the man or woman on whom others can always rely to get the job done, *Live by the List.* It will never fail you. Sometimes the most simple tasks are the most important.

The items so far suggested for your list are the routine actions you would put on your list in the course of your day's work, the tasks *others* expect you to do.

In addition, there are the things *you* think you should be doing to advance your own progress; books you should be reading to improve your expertise in certain skills; people you would like to meet who could become valuable contacts; meetings and seminars where subjects pertaining to your work are discussed and innovative ideas are introduced. New ideas and techniques for achieving your ambitions. Put them all on your list; otherwise time will go by and they will be overlooked.

There are other memory joggers.

Date books. Let's look in on a board of directors meeting of a large savings and loan association in Los Angeles. All thirty members of the board are gathered around the long boardroom table. A full list of important matters has just been completed, and the chairman of the board is ready to adjourn the meeting.

"There's one more item on the agenda," he says, "the date of the next meeting. It will be held in this room at ten A.M. on Tuesday morning, October sixth."

It's a pretty safe bet that all thirty of those directors are going to reach into their pockets, almost in unison, and bring out their little black date books. It's highly unlikely that any businessman who has reached that level would even think of leaving his home or office without his pocket appointment book. Certainly they have secretaries with bigger, more complete appointment calendars at the office, but any top-flight leader is much too busy, too involved in too many activities to rely on memory for future important dates. Carrying a date book may seem elementary, but it is one of the tremendous trifles that go into the making of leadership and efficiency.

Memory improvement is not one of the standard courses offered in most college curriculums, but its significance can hardly be overstated. Memory is the basis of all accumulated knowledge. We only *know* what we remember, but, sadly, most of us forget about 80 percent of all the information that is given to us during a lifetime. Anything you do to improve your memory can be confidently added to the asset section of your personal balance sheet.

THE BOTTOM LINE

1. Research indicates that *good memory* is one of the traits that top executives consider a bankable asset in the making of a successful career.

2. Modern psychology has proved that almost everyone's memory can be improved by using the new techniques.

3. Most major cities have professionals who offer courses in mnemonics, courses that teach scientific techniques that will eradicate the unintentional shortcomings that may be affecting your career.

4. "Living by the list," a daily scheduling of work that is created by you alone, is a fail-safe memory jogger that can bring instantaneous gratification.

5. Always carry your date book.

12

EASY DOES IT— EVERY TIME!

I love the man that can smile in trouble, that can gather strength from distress, and grow brave by reflection. 'Tis the business of little minds to shrink, but he whose heart is firm, and whose conscience approves his conduct, will pursue his principles unto death.

—THOMAS PAINE

There is a fine old word in this language of ours that should be a ready part of every top-flight executive's vocabulary—and of the *character* he brings to his work. The word is *imperturbability,* easily one of the most expressive words in Mr. Webster's dictionary.

Ernest Hemingway defined guts as "grace under pressure." The identical definition might also be given for imperturbability. *Imperturbability* is the state of being calm in the face of all manner of trouble and difficulty—of being unexcitable, unflappable, steady, and even-tempered no matter what chaos is raging about you. The state of imperturbability enables you to stand tall and think straight despite the pressure.

While a professor at the University of Pennsylvania, the great Canadian physician Sir William Osler told his medical students, "No quality ranks with imperturbability. It is *the* essential bodily virtue. Imperturbability means coolness of mind under all circumstances—calmness amid storm, clearness of judgment in moments of grave peril. Imperturbability is a blessing to you and a comfort to all who come in contact with you."

The Canadian-born Regius Professor of Medicine at England's Oxford University had reason to appreciate the state of imperturbability. The late Sir William was generally recognized as the world's most knowledgeable researcher in the field of stress and its causes. His teachings about stress in England, Canada, and the United States strongly influenced scientific thinking around the world.

An Inability to Cope Wrecks Career

Even if you are gifted with inordinate qualities of leadership, you will be unable to rise to the top until you learn to cope with the unexpected demands and pressures that go hand in hand with outstanding achievement. The case history of a man we'll call Robert C. Fulton clearly demonstrates that fact.

Robert C. Fulton seemed to be one of those "can't possibly miss" individuals when he was graduated from college. He had been elected to Phi Beta Kappa in his junior year, was graduated summa cum laude, and was filled with ideas for the betterment of mankind. Even his extracurricular activities proved that he had all the special qualities for success. He was the proverbial "big man on campus"—starting quarterback on the varsity football team and even president of his class. It was no wonder that his fellow students selected him as the man most likely to succeed.

Bob was a science major. He was eagerly recruited before graduation, and he joined the staff of a major oil company immediately afterward. His scientific training helped him make rapid progress, one promotion following another until he caught the attention of the big bosses upstairs. Word went around the shop that young Fulton was the fair-haired boy, in line for the top job at some point down the road if he behaved himself.

But something happened to Bob under the glare of the spotlight. There were disturbing incidents, evidence of abrasive personality traits that seemed out of keeping with his early behavior at school and on the job. Several times he lost his "cool" and clashed with his superiors, actually telling them off. An explosion at a tank farm in his territory caused something to snap inside Fulton with equally destructive force. There was heavy property loss, and a number of workers were injured. Bob couldn't stand the effect of this extra stress and pressure. He lost control completely, panicked, and began to run away from all his responsibilities.

After that disastrous explosion, Bob became supersensitive to every kind of criticism. His unnecessary belligerence caused his subordinates to describe him as a man with a short fuse. His relations with his men soured and he lost their respect. In time, his personnel file at headquarters contained a notation that he often became insubordinate and insisted on doing things his way rather than the way prescribed by the company

As if predestined to write the final scene of a theatrical tragedy, top management reluctantly felt there was no choice but to let him go. It was a perfect time for Fulton to reevaluate his personal problems and his career, but he failed to do so. His admirable quality of singleness of purpose secured him new employment, but he seemed unable or unwilling to change the weakness in his makeup. He had fallen into the trap of losing control of himself in stressful situations, of being unable to take constructive criticism without showing instant resentment. He went on from one job to another, always terminated for the same reasons. He had fallen from "crown-prince–apparent" of his company to a man with the reputation of someone who couldn't hold a job.

The very nature of our existence has proved again and again that there can be no truly *indispensable* man. No individual, no matter how talented or ambitious he may be, can achieve or retain real success until he learns to control himself under pressure. Or as Daniel Defoe put it, "The height of human wisdom is to *make a calm within*, under the weight of *the greatest storm without.*" When the world describes someone by saying "He just couldn't stand success," they might as easily be saying he never learned the value of imperturbability. *Executive Health Report* for December 1984 notes that

> In his book *The Anatomy of Courage*, Lord Moran, Winston Churchill's personal physician during World War II, tells the story of an admirable young officer named Hill. Moran's account goes back to the First World War, at the battle of Ypres. Moran

writes that D Company was hit by a terrifying German bombardment that left every one of the unit's officers wounded, except Hill. Hill was sleeping in his dugout during the artillery attack when a direct hit on his position caused the bulwarks to collapse on top of him. Miraculously, Hill was extricated safely, looking none the worse for wear. Not in the least rattled, he coolly took command of the company and received a battlefield promotion.

A fellow officer gave Lord Moran a revealing glimpse into Hill's makeup shortly after that incident. "Hill is only 28," the man said, "but you feel you can *rely* upon him. He's always the same sane and levelheaded person—the last man to do anything foolish on the spur of the moment or from impulse." Romanticists have said that war brings out the most admirable qualities in men, but it seems likely that young Hill had those qualities all along, if we're to accept the judgment of his fellow officer.

Train Yourself for Imperturbability

Is it possible to develop imperturbability within yourself, even if you come from a long line of hot-tempered, emotional people? The answer to the question is an emphatic yes! That is not to suggest that you want to turn yourself into an unfeeling automaton. The secret lies in learning to *control* these emotions that can harm you. Psychology has come up with answers to the problem, answers based on scientific studies.

William James, one of the founders of modern psychology, makes this observation:

We feel sorry *because* we cry, angry *because* we strike, afraid *because* we tremble; and *not* that we cry, strike or tremble because we are sorry, angry or fearful. . . . Refuse to express emotion and it dies. Count to ten before venting your anger and its occasion seems ridiculous. . . . Whistling to keep up your courage is no mere figure of speech. . . . If we wish to conquer undesirable emotional tendencies we must assiduously go through the *outward movements* of those contrary dispositions which we prefer to cultivate. The reward of persistency will infallibly come!

James's point, made many years ago, is very well taken. How many times have you heard someone say, "The more I think about it, the madder I get"? In other words, we actually force our undesirable emotions and must concentrate on the opposite action in order to overcome them. If we deliberately attempt to *act* calmly during the moments of greatest stress, real calmness will take over and extricate us from the crisis. The old story of a little boy "whistling in the graveyard to keep his courage up" has a sound psychological basis. Professor James's early pronouncements on this subject have been confirmed recently by a scientific study conducted at the University of California by Dr. Paul Ekman and associates. This study reveals that the act of flexing the facial muscles to indicate anger or joy actually produces these emotions in human beings.

Analyzing anger. There's an old wives' tale that anger turns inward if it isn't immediately vented. Supposedly, this can lead to ulcers and all manner of physical and psychological problems. This theory is now being denied by the experts. Dr. Carol Tavris, author of the book *Anger: The Misunderstood Emotion,* says, "People who are most prone to give vent to their rage *get angrier,* not less angry." Dr. Tavris further states that expressed anger often produces full-scale warfare, because one person's anger is a threat to another and *provokes* anger in return. Therefore, the best thing to do is nothing at all. After the heat of the moment has passed, the incident itself may turn out to be of no consequence. Remaining silent gives you time to study the situation coolly to see whether anything at all needs to be said or done.

Analzying fear. The experts agree that walking away from fear is the worst possible way to exorcise it. You are better served when you embrace fear—discover exactly what causes it—or the fear will simply grow worse. The reasoning behind this theory is simple: familiarity breeds contempt, of *fear* as well as of other things. Imagine the very worst happening to you as a result of your facing a particular fear, and you will usually discover that the actuality is far less severe than the fear itself. The childhood dread of a visit to a dentist is a perfect example of this. Fear is the mechanism that oftentimes transforms itself into open belligerence or anger, because we don't know how to cope with it. Learn to understand it—face it—and you will be well on your way to acquiring imperturbability.

Analyzing stress. Subconscious anger and fear, even more than your work load, are the primary breeders of inner stress. Fear of failure causes us to become supersensitive, ready to flare back in open anger at even

the mildest constructive criticism. With these two unhealthy emotions feeding off each other, we build a destructive pressure that stealthily overcomes us and takes
away our abilities to think clearly. The individual who
allows himself to become a stress casualty is akin to the
fine horse and jockey that must carry extra weight: it
becomes an *unnatural handicap* that must get in the
way of pure *performance.*

What We Can Do About It

From a purely material viewpoint, the human body is an
awesomely complex machine. Like any fine machine,
each of its parts must be doing its proper share of the
work for the whole to achieve peak performance. In recent years we have seen vivid proof that physical exercise is tremendously beneficial to the nervous system
and the entire thinking process. There is now no doubt
that regular workouts make the body far less sensitive to
stress. Exercise releases endorphins, the body's calming
chemicals that give a person a sense of well-being.

A visit to a big-city street or a quiet country lane in
the early morning hours anywhere in America reveals
that an extraordinary something has happened to our
society within the past fifteen years. People are *running.*
Men and women who run several miles a day claim this
exercise is euphoric, almost *addictive.* It has become one
of the best methods of relieving stress. One Park Avenue
psychiatrist in New York City has been able to calm potential suicides with a simple suggestion. He tells them

to go outside and run around the block as fast as they can before reporting back to his office. When they return, breathing heavily and relaxed by the sudden exertion, suicide is almost always completely out of their minds.

If you carry heavy responsibilities and find yourself in constant stressful situations, try exercise for relief. Running or jogging or walking rapidly cost nothing and require no advance scheduling. Calisthenics can be done in your office, in your home, or in a nearby gym if you prefer company. The most beneficial type of exercise is aerobic, one that requires some exertion that will raise your pulse rate and demand rapid deep breathing. Tennis, badminton, squash, and basketball are especially effective and the best exercise of all is swimming laps. Golf and other such games are of minimal value as exercise because they require insufficient exertion. By the same token, weightlifting will develop your muscles but it cannot be considered an aerobic exercise and will not add one year to your life.

A good program of aerobic exercises will go far toward relieving the symptoms of stress, and careful thinking and planning will help bring you up to the level of imperturbability. Dale Carnegie advised people oppressed by anxiety and fear to live in what he called "day-tight compartments." His theory was that we should dismiss the problems of *yesterday,* stop thinking of the problems of *tomorrow,* and live for *today only.*

English novelist Storm Jameson held similar views: "I believe that only one person in a thousand knows the trick of really living in the present. Most of us spend fifty-nine minutes an hour living in the past with regret for lost joys, or shame for things badly done (both utterly useless and weakening) or in a future we either long for or dread. The only way to live is to accept each minute as an unrepeatable miracle, which is exactly what it is—a miracle, and unrepeatable."

Viewed in this context, each day of our lives takes on such a special meaning that greeting it with any emotion stronger than joyful anticipation would be downright *sinful.* Imperturbability is such an important and achievable character trait because, without it, we have little control over the baser emotions that can propel us toward failure, in our careers and our personal lives.

Few writers or experts on human behavior have been able to define the advantages of imperturbability better than English poet laureate Rudyard Kipling more than fifty years ago. The first and last stanzas of his poem "If" say it all with strength and dignity:

If you can keep your head when all about you
Are losing theirs and blaming it on you;
If you can trust yourself when all men doubt you,
But make allowance for their doubting too;
If you can wait and not be tired by waiting,
Or being lied about, don't deal in lies,
Or being hated, don't give way to hating,
And yet don't look too good, nor talk too wise:

If you can talk with crowds and keep your virtue,
Or walk with Kings—nor lose the common touch,
If neither foes nor loving friends can hurt you,
If all men count with you, but none too much;
If you can fill the unforgiving minute

With sixty seconds' worth of distance run,
Yours is the Earth and everything that's in it,
And—which is more—you'll be a Man, my son!

THE BOTTOM LINE

1. A conscious decision to develop a state of imperturbability is the harried person's trusted defense against a host of problems and an invaluable aid to clear thinking.

2. Anger and fear are the chief wreckers of bright careers. Imperturbability will enable you to think and avoid destructive temper flare-ups and help you face your fears head on.

3. A dedicated program of aerobic exercise is a proven cure for the most harmful effects of stress.

13

EMPATHY: A TRAIT WITH HIDDEN BENEFITS

Utmost decency, in all our dealings with the other fellow, is the greatest need of the hour. Isn't he just you and me? Besides, being the proper thing, in the long run, it pays handsome dividends.

—ALBERT B. LORD

Empathy is another of those words in the English language that has slowly evolved into something it was not originally designed to be. It is too often thought to be almost interchangeable with a similar word, *sympathy*. Its actual, unvarnished definition is "The capacity for participation in another's feelings or ideas." That makes it one of those often overlooked human qualities that can be of immense value to any individual who aspires to great success.

In *To Kill a Mockingbird*, novelist Harper Lee has one of her characters say: "You never really understand a person until you consider things from his point of view—until you climb into his skin and walk around in it." The Sioux people of the Dakotas, with no written language, orally passed along a similar but more spiritual saying from generation to generation: "You will never understand another until you have walked a mile in his moccasins."

Empathy, and the ability to be empathetic, certainly can be greatly concerned with the spiritual side of human existence. Attempting to understand the feelings of others, feelings that have little to do with our own experience, can make us more tolerant and loving human beings. And that is all to the good. However, as this book is primarily concerned with the art of *self-management,* let's examine the hidden, very practical benefits that are part and parcel of learning to be empathetic. If you really want to influence people and bring them around to your own point of view, the quality of *empathy* is one of the most useful aids you can take with you to the marketplace.

Making It Work for You

Alexander Baker was a young lawyer in Arizona back in 1913 before that western territory was admitted to statehood. He was a remarkably successful trial lawyer, winning case after case, often when neither the facts in his case nor the law was entirely on his side. Alex Baker possessed a pleasing personality and a shrewd knowledge of the law. He was a hard worker with an insatiable thirst for victory. But Baker always credited his ability to empathize as his most useful character trait. He practiced empathy while he practiced law. He used empathy successfully to win over judges and juries to his line of reasoning.

"I spend twice as much time," he once said, "studying the arguments I believe *my opponent* will present in court as I do in preparing my own case. In my mind, I pretend that I have been employed by my opponent's client to present his case for him. I mentally put myself in his place, as if I were his lawyer. I get all the facts and look up the law on his side. Then I sit down and prepare his case, so when I go into court, I know in advance every argument he will bring up and how to refute each one of them, as well as knowing the arguments on my own side of the case."

Alexander Baker was *empathetic*. This learned skill proved to be the most effective weapon he carried into the courtroom. In fact, it worked so well for him that Alexander Baker became the first chief justice of the Arizona Supreme Court when that territory finally became the forty-eighth state in the Union.

It's important to recognize that no one is *born* with this skill. Because *self-preservation* is generally considered the first "law" of human nature, it seems obvious that taking the time to concern oneself with the feelings and ideas of *others* takes more than a little concentration and willpower. Fortunately, in a civilized society, enlightened parental and religious teaching (not to mention the force of law) give us good reason to refrain from absolute self-centeredness. Empathy is a double-edged sword for *good*—the beginning of a completely altruistic quest to be a more decent person, and a digging device that will enable you to tunnel into the most private thinking of an erstwhile opponent and "turn" him to your side.

Without intending to lessen the spiritual application of empathy, let's concentrate on its purely practical uses. If you were a bit surprised to discover that a determined trial lawyer might concern himself with being empathetic, can you believe that a Vince Lombardi or a Mike Ditka might consider empathy at all important in such a violent sport as football? Actually, success in most competitions calls for a high degree of empathy. Every winning football coach and every outstanding quarterback who calls his own plays must be empathetic. Neither can hope to penetrate the opponents' defense unless he tries to outthink the opposition, to be empathetic with the other side to the point that he has a good idea of what they'll try next.

Empathy, used in this manner, plays an important role in every walk of life—from social bridge playing to concern for our parents to romantic love to business. It is virtually impossible to show our interest in another human being or to have any influence with that person unless we make an attempt to understand his or her feelings and ideas. Consider the salesman, on whatever level, whose entire career depends on his ability to secure more "yeas" than "nays." Every salesman who brings in more than his share of the orders does so by first convincing his potential customer that he is as concerned about the needs of the *client* as he is about the commission dollars he'll earn from making the sale.

How to Develop Empathy

Like all of the positive character traits that are the keys to the art of self-management, developing empathy must begin with your own private thought processes.

Have you, to this point, previously considered the built-in advantages of empathy? Do you already possess it to a certain degree? Have you ever achieved any measure of success by employing it on your own behalf?

Empathy is one of the vital skills every achiever has mastered, and it is the keystone of good human relations. To make it work for you, you must become a kind of "mind reader," someone who has the powers of clairvoyance. There need be nothing mysterious or magical about that power. The word comes from the French verb *voir*, which means "to see clearly." A good measure of homework, even "cramming," will supply you with all the clairvoyant powers you will need. Begin your quest for empathy by following these generalized rules:

1. Test your instinctive powers of empathy by selecting someone with whom you totally disagree. In your own mind, try to find some understandable reasoning behind his actions, feelings, or ideas.

2. Become a *listener.* Only by paying close attention to the conversation of others can you have any immediate understanding of the depth of their feelings or the strength of their ideas.

3. Prepare *beforehand.* When you enter a meeting with an individual or a group who are important to your personal goals, you should have thoroughly briefed yourself with all the information available on them, their company, their needs, and their ambitions.

4. Even when you are in an adversarial position, it is always wise to have a good grasp of your opponent's point of view. You will then be prepared to counter his best moves and defeat him or, by gentle persuasion and logic, win him over to your side.

The practical applications of empathy are virtually limitless. Many people fail to win the job or promotion they desperately want because they "put the cart before the horse." They forget that the person who interviews them cares less about what he can do for them than about what *they* can do for *him!* The next time you appear for such an interview, use your skills of empathizing and place yourself on the other side of the desk in your imagination. What qualities, what experience, what skills would *you* want from an employee? If you present your case in those terms, you'll get a more respectful hearing and improve your chances of landing the job.

At the same time, a thorough knowledge of the power of empathy can be used to persuade others to be empathetic with you. The most quoted line in President John F. Kennedy's inaugural speech was the stirring "And so, my fellow Americans, ask not what your country can do for you; ask what you can do for your country." With those few challenging words he elevated himself above the politics of promise and inspired thousands of talented Americans to volunteer for the Peace Corps, through which they could improve their homeland's image by good works in underdeveloped nations around the globe.

From a purely practical viewpoint, empathy is one of the most useful skills any leader can master. If you have developed the capacity for empathy and the ability to use it, you will find your managerial chores far less complicated. In any business, the head man or woman must win the loyalty and support of employees to encourage maximum production. Often a manager finds that various people in the chain of command have personalities and ideas that are diametrically opposed. The effective leader must be empathetic—able to perceive and appreciate the conflicting viewpoints, find common ground for agreement, and bring them all together under his or her leadership.

To some, the traits of being empathetic and having singleness of purpose might seem contradictory. They are not. The person who aspires to greatness in his field never allows himself to lose sight of his ultimate goal. That is singleness of purpose. That same individual quickly learns the hidden advantages of empathy. By learning and trying to understand the feelings and ideas of others, he prepares himself for the inevitable rockfalls along the way and discovers a much smoother ascent to the summit.

If we are to believe the cynics, selfishness is a major component of all of us. Developing the practice of searching out the motivations of people with whom you disagree is not an easy task. But once you establish this excellent habit, you will have acquired a priceless skill, and you will have become a better *person* in the process.

THE BOTTOM LINE

1. Empathy is not only a positive character trait, beloved by humanists, but a learnable skill that can help you achieve success.

2. On the athletic field and in the business world, the ability to feel empathy enables you to anticipate your opponent's moves and turn them to your own advantage.

3. You can enhance your instinctual empathy by practice; try to understand the views of those with whom you have little in common; *listen* closely to others; secure advance information about the feelings and ideas of those with whom you plan to confer.

4. An outward display of empathy toward anyone with whom you deal is a simple but highly flattering indication that you value his feelings and ideas. It will automatically encourage your opposite number to reply in kind.

14

ON FRIENDS AND SUCCESS

Any one who has had a long life of experience is worth listening to, worth emulating, and worth tying to as a friend. No one can have too much experience in any line of endeavor. We readily welcome to our group of friends that one who talks with the voice of experience and common sense. We know that we are safe in his hands. He is not going to get us into trouble. Rather is he going to point out the pitfalls and mistakes that experience has taught him to avoid.

—GEORGE MATTHEW ADAMS

If you have the ability to become a friend to someone—an abundance of positive qualities that would make a person want to be your friend—you have already made a giant step forward in your drive to become an achiever.

In the last century a young man in London found himself in dire financial circumstances. He sorely needed a loan to stave off bankruptcy. This man had strong character and many worthwhile qualities. His only major flaw was the shyness that kept him from making friends easily. He had no one to turn to in his hour of need, and he became obsessed with the idea that the one person who could rescue him was the head of the great English banking house, Baron Rothschild. He did not even know Baron Rothschild, but he became determined to bring his dream to reality.

After days of determined effort, he was finally able to arrange an appointment with the baron. He felt very apprehensive, but he knew he had nothing to lose. Rothschild listened to the young man's story and became so impressed with his visitor's persistence and practical plan for averting failure that he decided to help him. The help offered came in an entirely unexpected form.

"Young man," the baron said, "I won't give you the loan you ask for, but I will do something even better. I'll put my arm around your shoulder and walk you across the floor of the exchange."

This public demonstration of his "intimate friendship" with the great Rothschild was all the help the young man needed. His determination, his practical planning had indeed won him a new friend. This new friendship encouraged others to seek *his* friendship, and he suddenly had no lack of aid in solving his financial problems. At the eleventh hour, this individual knew that he could not succeed alone, and, in desperation, he abandoned his pride and timidity to ask for the help of another. He had proved the value of friends, especially friends in high places.

The men or the women who allow themselves to believe that total independence is a noble virtue make a grave mistake. They will eventually learn that friends can be valuable partners in their success. No success stories are complete without mention of the help their subjects received from others along the way—especially older friends, mentors, who took an interest in them, encouraged them, advised them, pushed them—even put opportunities in their way. Precious few painters, musicians, composers, writers, and other artists whom we admire today would ever have made it without the patrons who befriended them during their early struggles.

Almost four centuries ago the English poet John Donne penned some lines that drew a memorable word picture that remains clear today: "No man is an island, entire of itself: every man is a piece of the continent, a part of the main."

These words have been widely quoted ever since that time because they are as true today as they were three and a half centuries ago. To achieve, every person must have help, for we must all work with and through others. Therefore, the more friends you have, the more likely you are to achieve your goals. Make it your business to make friends! Remember, unless people in a position to help you know you and have an opportunity to observe you in action, they will have neither opportunity nor reason to extend the hand of friendship.

False Pride Is a Sorry Obstacle

Many of the most gifted people in all fields have a common problem: They find it difficult, if not impossible, to ask for help. It is a natural psychological shortcoming. To them, asking for help is akin to confessing to some embarrassing lack in either their intelligence or resourcefulness. Yet, those who have already attained positions of power and responsibility have no such qualms. They say, "I need all the help I can get!" To them, admitting they can't go it alone is a sign that they are pursuing their goals with confidence. They do not consider a request for help a stigma signifying weakness.

In a tennis school the coach was particularly interested in a young pupil who showed much promise. The young player was already a consistent winner among the juniors, and the coach felt that a lucrative future on the professional circuit was not beyond the realm of possibility. He gave the youngster this advice: "Always arrange matches with players who are better than you. You can't really learn anything from those you can beat. You can only profit from those whose play is superior to yours."

That advice is excellent, on a universal scale. Whatever your profession or occupation, always try to learn from the champs. If you want to be an achiever, always try to associate with the achievers. Only from them will you learn. Only through them will your rise to the top become easier.

You would be dead wrong to make the natural assumption that these older, successful leaders could not possibly be interested in you. Except for a few self-centered individuals, those people who were bright enough to reach the top are also bright enough to stay on the lookout for young men and women with real promise. Look at it this way—it is a real feather in their caps if they become known as pickers of winners. The best of them receive enormous satisfaction from extending a helping hand to those on the way up.

Methods to Meet the Top People

We all know that a U.S. Army private can't just barge into the office for a friendly chat with the commanding general. It's also unlikely you can obtain an appointment the first time out with the top brass in most organizations—at least, not without proper connections: Too many secretaries and executive assistants are employed to guard them, to protect their valuable time. You must make such a contact more adroitly.

You will already share areas of common interest with the person you hope to meet if you now occupy a middle-management position. This gives you an opportunity to try, in football terminology, something of an end-around play. You can usually make the contact you want with a classic flanking movement—meeting the "unreachable" man in a setting away from the job. One of the quickest and easiest of all ways to meet important people on a proper basis is through civic and charitable organizations. Although the word *joiner* has taken on an undeserved derisive connotation in recent years, the dictionary defines a joiner as "a gregarious or civic-minded person who joins many organizations." That seems a much fairer definition.

Look at the letterhead of most civic and charitable organizations, and it becomes obvious that they attract the most outstanding people in the community. The reason is simple: they provide useful services. Your willingness to take part in such activities is an indication of the breadth of your interests and the depth of your character. At the same time, working with such organizations throws you into close contact with many people you might not otherwise meet.

You should not enter this work for purely selfish reasons. You will find it will be time well spent. Organization fees and dues, like the expense of wardrobe and business entertaining, should be considered an investment in your career. Clubs provide conveniences such as rooms for overnight stays, fine dining and exercise facilities, and, more important, they can also become the long-term source of many close friendships and valuable contacts.

In the long run, all of the positive traits that will help you become an achiever will also enable you to widen your circle of influential friends. If you are enthusiastic, empathetic, and able to speak and write well, you will be a person who automatically attracts others. Sometimes the direct approach is the most natural way of winning a friendship. Eric John Wilson, who wrote *There Are No Strangers*, said he made the most friendships and important contacts simply by introducing himself with a cheery hello. His findings indicated that most people are reluctant to make the first advance to an interesting stranger but are willing to respond warmly once the ice is broken.

It is simply impossible to have *too many* friends. After all, the quality and quantity of your friendships are a real barometer of the impact you make in your im-

mediate society. A prisoner in solitary confinement has
no opportunity to broaden his experience or his influence. Don't keep your warmer nature locked in a cell;
keep it circulating like the most popular book in the
public library. Become open and outgoing, start moving
in the places where people you would like to meet con-
gregate, and you will soon have many opportunities to
make valuable new friends.

There are times when you might meet a person in a
most unlikely place who is prepared to help your career
moves. This happened not long ago to several ambitious
young people in Los Angeles. A junior executive in the
personnel department of a large bank in that California
metropolis was assigned the project of upgrading the
quality of his firm's new employees. His department's
previous sources were help wanted ads in the daily
papers, usually unemployed walk-ins off the street, and
recommendations from bank employees, often of their
relatives. The bank knew that better talent must be
available somewhere, and after studying the problem,
the junior executive came up with an innovative idea.
He started attending some evening classes in the business school of a local university.

He reasoned that among those willing to spend
time preparing themselves for better jobs he might be
able to find the type of young people his company
wanted to hire. He was not disappointed. He met many
serious young men and women, bright, articulate, already employed, and eager to improve their lot. Being
able to fraternize with them before, during, and after
class, he had time to make some sound judgments on the
best possibilities. Some of those he recommended now

hold important posts in the bank, and the junior executive is no longer *junior*. His creative approach to his
department's hiring practice won him promotion to
personnel director.

No matter how much effort we give our daily work,
it's wise to remember that success is not calculated on
an hourly basis. There are many places to meet the right
kind of new people in numbers, away from the workplace. There are now many social organizations in the
larger churches and synagogues, physical-fitness groups
and other athletic clubs, and organizations promoting
every kind of hobby from stamp collecting to bird-
watching. A bit of looking will enable you to find many
social organizations made up of bright people with
common interests. Join with the intention of taking a
really active part in everything—work on committees,
serve on the board, bring in new members—and the
club leaders will sit up and pay attention.

Depending upon your degree of seriousness, you
might even pay heed to the late Groucho Marx's famous
philosophy about joining a club: "I wouldn't join any
club that would have me!" Groucho knew what it was
all about: He wanted to move into higher circles.

Friendship Is Not a One-Way Street

The way to *have* a friend is to *be* a friend. It's likely that
the primary objection of those who hesitate to make influential friends is the fear that they will be considered
users. At the same time, no person who has achieved a

position of power is going to be long misled by insincerity. It is far more difficult to refuse a worthy individual's honest request for help than it is to sniff out a sycophant's unabashed social climbing.

Those who go out of their way to help other people without any thought of return make real and lasting friendships. A helping hand is never forgotten. When the opportunity presents itself, the one who received your help will be the first to come to your aid.

Walter Lantz, a New York stockbroker, enjoyed meeting people and making friends. He liked to keep in touch with his ever-growing number of friends and be aware of their concerns. The sudden illness of one of his friends left him very distraught and started him on a new project that was close to his heart. He learned of his friend's illness on a Friday evening and made up his mind to pay him a visit the next morning. A city with close to 8 million people can be a lonely place, especially on Saturday morning when most business offices are closed and a large part of the population has fled to the country. Walter visited his friend in his sickbed and was deeply touched by his obvious gratitude.

From that moment on, Lantz made it a habit to make the rounds of the hospitals every Saturday morning to visit any of his friends who happened to be patients. He did it solely because he sincerely cared for the people, and he found that the visits gave him equal pleasure. As it happened, it was also one of the few times he could spend significant time with some of them—especially those who were always difficult to reach and were usually away in the suburbs on weekends. Did his friends appreciate his thoughtfulness? It could be only a coincidence but when these people were looking for a trustworthy broker to handle their financial affairs, guess whom they contacted first.

The longer we live the more we realize that the people who want to help themselves can only do so by helping others. It's a basic law of success. People who begin by asking how they can find success solely within themselves are doomed from the start. The rewards go to people who have searched diligently for ways to help others.

One of the many successful individuals to use this principle was James Cash Penney, now better known as *the* J. C. Penney. The fabulous Mr. Penney, starting in 1902 with a small general merchandise store in Kemmerer, Wyoming, built a multibillion-dollar business empire on the inspirational principle of the golden rule. In fact, for years the Penney stores were called The Golden Rule Stores. It was Mr. Penney's unwavering faith in that principle—always treat the customer as you yourself would want to be treated—that made them grow and prosper.

But perhaps even more important was Mr. Penney's attitude toward his employees. In the first place, he did not like the word *employee,* preferring to treat everyone as something of a partner. He called them associates, and he devoted himself to treating them as he would want to be treated were their situations reversed. Most of all, he knew that by helping them make money, he would assure his own success.

Too many of us have an instinctive fear of "losing ourselves" through serving others although, in truth, it is the best way to *find* the real "self." Every achiever needs the help of others. The more friends you make, the easier your progress will be. And, looking beyond the practical aspects of this endeavor, you will find that making new friends makes your life far more interesting and worthwhile.

THE BOTTOM LINE

1. Your capacity for attracting friends of all ages may have a direct influence on your progress in your career.

2. If you have shaped yourself into a person who can *deliver*, as well as talk, the top people of your industry will be more accessible than you might think. Helping you helps them.

3. Active membership in civic, charitable, social, and trade organizations can lead to a rewarding expansion of your circle of interesting and influential friends. The necessary expenditure of time and money should be considered an investment in your career.

4. Friendship is a two-way street. You make a friend by being a friend. If you honestly give of yourself, in personal concern and professional skill, no one can consider you a user.

15

STAY FIT
AND USE
YOUR MOMENTUM

The joy of feeling fit physically is reflected in a clearer and more useful mind. You may read and study forever, but you come to no more important truthful conclusions than these two: 1. Take care of your body (eat and exercise properly), and your mind will improve. 2. Work hard, and be polite and fair, and your condition in the world will improve.
—EDWARD HOWE

A jumbo jetliner lifts off the runway at O'Hare Airport in Chicago and heads for San Francisco. It leaves the ground at an angle of almost forty-five degrees, levels off at thirty-three thousand feet altitude, and will arrive at its destination in a few hours. This same flight leaves O'Hare at the same time every day, and hundreds of other departures take place at airports across the United States en route to cities in this country and abroad. This familiar scene is an almost miraculous event—350 tons of metal propelling 350 passengers across the skies.

How does this aeronautical happening fit into a program of self-management? Handily, we hope. It takes great power to lift a huge airliner off the ground because *inertia,* the tendency of matter to resist any motion, must be overcome. It takes much less energy to keep it flying safely because the aircraft then rides on its *momentum,* the friendly force that gives it the impetus to keep moving. The point is that whether in airplane takeoffs or human endeavor, the same set of basic principles applies.

In starting a career that will carry you to the top, you must go through an agonizing personal struggle to overcome inertia. Once inertia is conquered, and if you continue to function at peak performance, momentum will help you arrive at the destination of your choice. You must continually nurture and protect that momentum or you will be faced with the problem of besting that inertia all over again. And never forget that determined people, like airplanes, can seldom plan on the strain of only one "takeoff." You must have a dependable energy source always at the ready to enable you to keep that drive to succeed.

Older men and women rarely need sales pitches about the benefits of maintaining their health and fitness. The passing years have ingenious ways of reminding them that the physical machinery isn't operating quite as smoothly as in earlier times. But the vigor and exuberance of youth, especially when harnessed to satisfying work, has a tendency to hew to the Scarlett O'Hara philosophy:"I'll worry about that tomorrow."

In organizing your life to become an achiever, you should give a high priority to *attaining* and *maintaining* a state of physical fitness. No matter how young you may be, it's wise to remember that real fitness does not necessarily come with the territory. Grenville Kleiser, quoted in *Forbes Scrapbook*, says, "A man's best ally in his quest for success is good health. Without it he can't stand the pace." An ancient Spanish proverb says much the same thing: "A man too busy to take care of his health is like a mechanic too busy to take care of his tools."

Health and fitness should be considered ever-ready tools in your personal success kit. They will enable you to make the adjustments for clearer thinking and provide the energy spark needed to overcome the letdown of temporary setbacks. The very last thing you want, when you finally reach your goal, is to be physically unable to tap your foot when the band starts playing. That is an unthinkable but ever-present danger, as a recent news story in Michigan demonstrates.

In 1983 General Motors announced its Saturn Project. According to GM Chairman Roger Smith, the project would not only result in a compact car built as inexpensively as its counterparts in Japan but would also pioneer some basic changes in the entire process of automobile manufacturing. One can only speculate on the number of hours Smith and the other top GM brass spent finding the right man to head this new project, one of the most important in the history of America's biggest automotive manufacturer.

In January 1985, General Motors announced that it had found its man. Joseph J. Sanchez, fifty-four years old, was named to head the Saturn Project. Sanchez was considered a relatively young man for such an awesome responsibility, but he had already proved himself as the general manager at Oldsmobile, one of GM's most successful divisions. Sanchez had *earned* the big new job. Yet, within days of the announcement that he had been chosen to run the Saturn Project, another news article reported that Mr. Sanchez had been stricken with a heart attack and rushed to the intensive-care unit of a Detroit hospital. A few days and two new heart attacks later, Joseph J. Sanchez was dead.

This intelligent, dedicated executive, in his prime, had died without experiencing the full joys of what should have been his greatest achievement. There is no way of determining the extent of Mr. Sanchez's involvement in a personal health and fitness program, but medical science has established that a combination of proper diet and exercise is doing much to prevent, and sometimes reverse, the degenerative disease that leads to coronaries and strokes. Quite obviously, these dangerous illnesses, and many others that are correctable, are not confined to "old age."

The pace and pressures that come with the executive suites of the business world often lead to health problems for our top leaders. Many men and women of great ability fail to achieve the ultimate goals they are capable of reaching because of recurrent sickness or deteriorating physical conditions. This is a personal tragedy for the individual and also a costly setback for the company that has spent much time and money preparing that achiever for a position of leadership. That is why good health habits are becoming an increasingly important requirement for employment in any well-paid job.

Some years ago, one of America's largest corporations established a physical therapy department under the direction of a professional therapist. It built an on-site gymnasium with complete exercise equipment including a running track. When the management invited members of its staff to participate in the fitness program, most of those who signed up were junior executives. The juniors were attracted by the running program and gradually added laps week after week until many of them were running four and five miles a day.

This was early in what has become known as "the fitness craze," and many of the older executives were puzzled by the enjoyment their colleagues seemed to be getting out of *running*. When they asked the junior executives why they had become so enthusiastic about such a painful exercise, all of them replied that running was *habit-forming*. Every one of them claimed it was a good habit, that it was an activity that was *euphoric*, that it gave them a great lift—a sense of elation and well being. One of them even volunteered, "It's better than three martinis!"

Every year more and more major corporations across the nation are building or expanding their in-house fitness programs. Now, everyone is encouraged—often offered special incentives—to participate. Companies still make certain their stress-prone top executives make regular trips to cardiovascular centers to check on their health, but the fitness boom now reaches down to nearly every level. Such companies as AT&T, Allied Corporation, Johnson & Johnson, Union Carbide, and Berol USA all back energetic fitness programs that save them, in many cases, as much as 45 percent a year in medical costs and reduce disability time, in some instances, by more than 20 percent per annum. Eighty-two percent of AT&T's employees who participate in its fitness program claim they are more productive as a result of it.

In former days the consensus opinion was that only athletes or those involved in actual physical labor had good reason to concern themselves with fitness. We now know better. *Anyone* planning to fly to success had better have his transportation in perfect working order or he'll never get off the ground.

How to Get Your Momentum Going

This chapter has been deliberately placed in this part of the book because the time will come, after you've mastered many of the techniques of self-management, when you'll feel bereft of the time and energy to continue their practice. In some ways, a lifelong dedication to becoming an achiever can be likened to one superlong and exhausting workday. It's important to pace yourself, without sloughing anything off, so you'll still be at your best for that make-or-break meeting in late afternoon.

That is where the ability to maintain your momentum will carry the day for you. Momentum can be attained only after you have overcome inertia. A good night's sleep is perhaps the most beneficial form of inertia we encounter on a natural level. To get their momentum going after sleep, many energetic men and women start their days with some form of vigorous physical exercise. Chicago sales executive Turner Munsell, now retired and living in Florida, found a foolproof way of overcoming the inertia that prompts many of us to say "I'll postpone exercise until later in the day when I'm more awake."

"I made up my mind," Munsell grins, "that I would *never* eat breakfast until *after* I had exercised. I get awfully hungry in the morning but, under my plan, I can't eat until I've taken my morning workout. Believe me, that works for me. Incidentally, it is always better to exercise before rather than after eating. You should start by doing only a few exercises when you first begin your morning workouts. Then add to the number each week until you reach the optimum number and feel you're getting the full benefit—when you have a real sense of elation."

Mr. Munsell's plan has worked well for him and it offers a practical device that could aid you. If the prospect of improved health and vitality isn't enough to keep you going in the beginning of your personal fitness program, try the "reward-punishment" system. The beginning of any self-improvement program is always the most difficult. Changing your eating habits to the norm now generally prescribed by nutritionists and health professionals may also be tough for the first three or four weeks. After that, a majority of sensible dieters report their state of health and energy has improved so greatly that they plan to continue the program indefinitely.

Those who have been successful in ridding themselves of other bad habits, including excessive drinking and smoking, also reveal that the first few days are the most difficult. Alcoholics Anonymous uses this illustration: Alcoholics who stop drinking are like riders on a train. When they stop drinking, they get off at a station some distance from where they started. If they start drinking again, they get back on the train at the same station where they got off. In other words, they return to the same stage of alcoholism they were in when they decided to give it up.

Again, attaining the power of momentum requires little more than replacing bad habits with a thought-out system of *good* habits. If you are determined to be an achiever, here are three rules that will help you power your way there:

1. Study the facts and make a conscious decision to alter your methods.

2. The early stages of your new approach will be the most difficult. Prepare to "sweat them out."

3. Seize the advantage of the first twinges of success and go with it. Momentum is about to take over.

The need to prepare your physical entity for the labor and stress it will encounter on your way to the top deserves as much attention as the care you have taken to prepare your mind. There are innumerable books on diet, health, and fitness that will serve you well. Enlightening publications from the U.S. Government Printing Office are also available for the asking. *Momentum* will help safeguard your personal fuel supply, and no difficult journey is ever pleasant if the "transportation" isn't working well.

Don't Lose It—Use It!

"What you don't use, you lose." That is a succinct saying that John Paul Floyd, a retired U.S. Navy officer living in Washington, D.C., recalls his grandmother's telling him when he was a young lad. In fact, his grandmother explained that it had been passed along from generation to generation in her family. In recent years medical science has proved that the nonuse of vital organs in the elderly and others really *does* lead to deterioration. That is one of the reasons prolonged bed rest and hospitalization are fast becoming things of the past.

Concern about losing what you don't use is a philosophy with valid significance for would-be achievers. When momentum is lost, there's a strong danger that it will be replaced ultimately by *atrophy.* That is an argument, made in colorful style, by a man named Robert Townsend—undeniably one of the greatest achievers in American business in this century. Townsend earned an enviable reputation as a revitalizer of troubled companies when he held top positions in such firms as Avis Rent-A-Car, 20th Century–Fox, American Express, and Dun and Bradstreet.

In his book *Further Up the Organization* (1984) Townsend offered these straight-from-the-shoulder explanations to explain his theory of "Why big-company CEOs aren't leaders":

> Because they stopped taking chances when they got in line for the top job. And because the rewards of the top job make it impossible to lead. . . . After a few months of this, you've lost touch with all the colleagues who helped you get the job, and you have no idea what's going on. . . . How about the next layer of management? They've all reached the golden escalator where noses are clean, voices subdued, records unbesmirched by mistakes, and the key word is WAIT. In fact, there is no leadership. The

top corporate staff are presiding over the remaining *momentum* through their mastery of the techniques of meeting and report writing—all in the service of not rocking the boat.

Those are strong words and, agree with them or not, they do pinpoint some of the chief killers of momentum. It can only be sustained if you have the desire and the physical ability to stay in the middle of the battle. Because of this, many top executives have devised ingenious methods of keeping their momentum operating at full pitch to forestall atrophy. Some achievers find that long vacations interrupt their work too much and interfere with their momentum. They deliberately settle for three or four shorter vacations at different seasons of the year. Others bypass formal vacations altogether and operate year-round on a four-day week. They never permit themselves to be away from the throttle for more than three days at a time. Still others, when they feel the need of a vacation, work on a half-day schedule until they've regained their strength.

If we feel, as we should, that the work we do is far more than just a means to a paycheck, then our struggle to maintain the momentum that keeps us on an arrow-straight course is worth whatever effort it takes. John Miller had these interesting thoughts on struggle: "Nature everywhere has written her protest against idleness; everything which ceases to struggle, which remains inactive, rapidly deteriorates. It is the struggle toward an ideal, the constant effort to get further, which develops manhood and character."

Very few things come easily to all people, but the ones who keep trying are the ones who make it. One of life's most jarring moments comes, usually past the age of thirty-five, when you look into your mirror and see the face of a middle-aged person. The face looks familiar, but there are noticeable wrinkles and sags that didn't seem to be there before. Is it all over—time to pack for the big downhill slide? Not at all, according to an energetic achiever named Jane Fonda. In her book *Women Coming of Age*, Ms. Fonda writes:

> For better or worse, all that has come before begins to come of age in midlife—our eating habits, our exercise patterns, whether we smoke, the way we've generally lived our lives. If we've been living in the fast lane, ignoring our own physical and psychological needs, we'll be aging in the fast lane as well, speeding toward the stereotype of declining vitality in midlife. But rarely is it too late to switch tracks. We each have the ability to slow the aging process. It's even possible that we can physically improve with age. If we're not at our maximum level of fitness, which few of us are, there is actually room to make ourselves healthier and in some cases stronger than in our early adulthood.

There can be a tendency for human beings to decide at some point in their lives that they have made their contribution and are now entitled to sit back, relax, and live on their past successes. For some, this comes with retirement. For others, it comes when they finally move into the executive office they have had their eyes on for years. In either case, that tendency can be fatal—physically and intellectually. No one can win this year's ball games with last year's scores. What was done in the past is no longer significant. Only a successful *today* can lead to a future filled with promise. Each goal attained should be considered a stepping stone to new and greater achievements tomorrow.

Some advice from *Bits and Pieces* makes the point beautifully:

> When you feel you've got it made, watch out! It's the first step toward settling back into a pleasant convenient rut. People who have it "made" are only one step from being has-beens. Like anyone who coasts, there's only one place for them to go— downhill. Keep alive, keep challenging yourself until the day you quit. When growth stops, decay begins. Keep exercising your muscles. Keep exercising your brain.

All the organs and muscles of your body work in conjunction with your brain to keep you functioning and productive. One of your first duties is to keep the entire package working smoothly. Remember, it's much easier to maintain your momentum than to stop and start again. In other words: keep on keeping on!

THE BOTTOM LINE

1. Few successful companies are willing to fill really important positions with anyone whose health might interfere with his performance.

2. An active program of physical fitness and proper diet provides the energy necessary to harness the momentum that will propel you to your goals.

3. Momentum can be utilized only after a thoughtful decision to recognize its value, a willingness to suffer through the early stages of attaining it, and an ability to seize the proper moment to switch to full throttle.

4. The successful leader never willingly permits the level of the momentum he has created to slacken. He recognizes it as his lifeline. If it falls too low, atrophy and failure follow.

16

MOVE UP TO *CREATIVE* THINKING

All workers in the world could be divided into just two classes, the work *processors* and the *creative thinkers.*

—ROBERT JENKINS

Examine the accomplishments of any successful person—in any field you can think of, however uncerebral—and it becomes apparent that a great deal of careful *thought* went into the making of that career. Then examine the achievements of any *giant* in a field where thinking is a prerequisite, and it becomes apparent that *something extra* went into the making of that career. That additional quality necessary for great achievement has now been defined as a process called *creative thinking.*

155

The late Bob Jenkins of Binghamton, New York, the chief executive of a large corporation, often said that all the workers in the world could be divided into two categories—the *work processors* and the *creative thinkers.* He claimed that the work processors busy themselves all day processing work that flows across their desks, simply attempting to keep their daily output up to schedule. Unlike the creative thinkers, in Mr. Jenkins's equation, they give little time to questioning what they are doing, why they are doing it, or in what way the system might be improved.

That seems an apt description of a situation that is all too familiar, at every level of the work chain. The work processor will put in his time and do a dependable job, but he cannot hope for major advancement and responsibility. It will be the creative thinker who breaks out of the pack.

Why are there so many of the one type and so few of the other? One way to find out is to take a look at the average executive and the way he spends his day. In the morning his desk is covered with letters that must be answered, phone calls that must be returned, subordinates waiting to report to him, and committee meetings to attend. He then takes time out for a possibly productive business lunch and returns to his office to start the same process all over again. Before he knows it, his day is over. He has been *busy* every moment, but he has taken little if any time to think about the real problems confronting him and the company that pays his salary.

This is not to say that most executives are lacking in creative ability, but only to demonstrate that most of them are unable to add a time for creative thinking to their list of important things to do. Most of them are so busy putting out fires they have no time to think about how they might have prevented them from occurring in the first place. They end up spending their valuable time running from crisis to crisis.

There is no doubt that the truly creative thinkers are a distinct minority unto themselves. They are the men and women who *make* the time to question the old way of doing things, the people who believe that no matter how long something has been done only one way, it is possible to find a better way of doing it. They are the leaders who find bright new methods to increase sales, cut costs, develop new products, strengthen personnel, and finance growth. They make any organization an exciting place to be.

The encouraging information for any potential achiever is that this valuable, thinking worker doesn't always come from the corporation's top brass. The innovator sometimes can be even a pieceworker on the assembly line, a salesman making calls in the field, or a clerk distributing messages from the mail room. Such people are often closer to the operating problems of the organization than the isolated chiefs on the top floor.

Creative thinking can clear the way for bright people on lower levels to move up eventually, but the real innovators are more immediately concerned with the valid bottom-line contributions they can make to the company. The personal satisfaction they derive from the knowledge that they have made a *difference* can be fantastic. That kind of thinking, in itself, will lead to more material rewards.

Do You Measure Up?

If you have never thought of yourself in terms of either work processor or creative thinker, this might be an excellent time to do so. Think about it. Have you come up with an innovation that improves the way you have been doing things on your job? Here is a brief quiz you can give yourself right now:

1. What am I doing on the job that I shouldn't be doing?

2. What should I be doing that I am not doing?

Honest, thoughtful answers to these two simple questions may give you an indication of how you rate. Native intelligence, the best education, and even the best intentions are all wonderful tools for any achiever, but they don't always ensure an aptitude for creative thinking—as the following story reveals.

Several years ago, Stanley Jarman, the founder and chief executive officer of Genesco, personally hired a young man who was a product of an excellent graduate school of business. Jarman thought this particular individual had the right stuff to become a top executive of the company someday. He arranged for the young man to spend three months in the head office, rotating through the various departments—manufacturing, sales and advertising, finance, accounting, and so on. He was to receive a cram course on the real basics of the shoe business.

At the end of the first month Mr. Jarman asked his protégé to come to his office and report on what he had learned. Feeling quite proud of himself and his business school background, the young man delivered a lengthy report to his chief on all the things he had found wrong with the operation. It was a veritable laundry list of criticisms. Mr. Jarman listened attentively and, when the newcomer had finished, asked him whether he was certain he had nothing more to add. When the visitor said he thought he had pretty well covered everything from his viewpoint, Jarman leaned back and studied him for a very long moment.

"Young man," he said finally, "never, ever come in my office again with a criticism of the way we do things here—unless first you have prepared a well-thought-out solution to each problem. *Anybody* can find problems. What we need here are solutions."

Obviously, in Mr. Jarman's opinion, his bright young man had mastered only the first piece of the puzzle—finding the problems. He neglected to think creatively about the solutions. Solutions to problems always call for creative thinking. Thomas Edison had a framed saying on his office wall, which read: "It is remarkable to what lengths people will go to avoid thought. That is tragically true. Some of us think, more of us think we think and most of us don't even think of thinking."

William F. Bramstedt, onetime president of California Texas Oil Co. Ltd., gave considerable thought to the subject of management's thinking.

Bramstedt places executives on three levels: those recalling and studying the past (such as comptrollers), those regarding and controlling the present (such as plant managers), and those contemplating and planning the future (such as presidents and vice-presidents). "Those chosen for top management," he said, "must be

of challenging, inquisitive mind, must be in great measure insulated from the history of the past and the routine of the present, and must, unlike the good soldier, be
constantly questioning *why*." In Bramstedt's opinion
such phrases as "hard to get to," "the man with the
clean desk," and "the fellow with his feet on the desk"
are perfect descriptions of what a chief executive should
be—*"providing he also thinks!"*

People often consider the time spent thinking as
time lost because they are not *physically* active, not
producing something tangible. That, of course, is a
throwback to the trusted values of the American work
ethic. But the real truth is that time spent in thinking
has ultimately produced all the great books, all the great
music, all the great inventions—all the great new ideas
and concepts that have changed the world. All truly
momentous achievements began as *thoughts* in someone's mind.

The greatest deterrent to the process of creative
thinking is the paucity of quiet time in which to do it. A
progressive architectural firm in Denver, Hoover Berg
Desmond, began a program to overcome that problem a
few years ago. Without informing the outside world, the
company instituted something called the "quiet hour"
between 10:00 and 11:00 A.M. every workday morning.
No telephone calls were accepted, no meetings sched-
uled, and the employees were encouraged to refrain
from talking to each other during that period. The idea
was to work and think *alone*, without distraction. After
more than three years of experience, partner Gary Desmond says, "I think an hour of quiet time is worth an
hour and a half of non-quiet time!"

We are all familiar with the Newton-apple-gravity

legend, and many other lasting discoveries were made in strange places and at unlikely times. Archimedes supposedly discovered the principle of buoyancy that bears his name while taking a bath, and George de Mestral came up with the idea for a product that would be called Velcro because of the burrs he was forced to remove from his dog's coat after a walk in the country. It's the *thinking* that counts, rather than the specific time or place.

Is Creative Thinking a Special Gift?

Officially, the jury is still out on the question of whether creativity is a gift, but many serious studies have proved that the skills of creative thinking can certainly be greatly enhanced, if not learned. A Massachusetts man named George M. Prince has spent more than twenty-five years trying to unlock the secrets of creative thinking. He believes most intelligent people have the ability to think creatively, but it is an ability they keep locked inside themselves because of fear. Companies such as Chase Manhattan Bank, IBM, Wang Laboratories, Gillette, Bank of Boston, and Digital Equipment have sent their employees to Prince's consulting firm, Synectics, Inc., in an effort to learn a more creative approach to their work.

Don Koberg and Jim Bagnall, teachers of creative problem solving at a California university, also maintain that creativity is a learnable behavior that anyone can develop. They feel that our society builds many barriers against the idea of being creative, barriers that induce fear. In their book, *The Universal Traveler: A Soft-Sys-*

tems Guide to Creativity, Problem-Solving, and the Process of Reaching Goals, they list ten of those fears:

1. Fear of making mistakes;
2. fear of being seen as a fool;
3. fear of being criticized;
4. fear of being misused;
5. fear of being "alone";
6. fear of disturbing tradition and making changes;
7. fear of being associated with "taboos";
8. fear of losing the security of habit;
9. fear of losing the love of the group; and
10. fear of truly being an individual.

That *fear* of creative thinking that Prince, Koberg, Bagnall, and others mention has always been with us, but there are those people who seem always to think creatively. Their thoughts gravitate naturally to solving problems. They enjoy the challenge of improving on the old ways of doing things. Solving problems is what makes their world tick, and much of what they contribute adds to the dimension of the lives of their fellowman. These special people have overcome any sense of fear they may have had and have replaced that emotion with vision. They are the creative thinkers responsible for new product lines, for better ways of doing things, hence developing our business, banking, and manufacturing at such a rapid rate that we are the envy of many nations.

Sandra Lawrence, director of new ventures at Gillette, never considered herself a creative person. She was sent by her company to Synectics, Inc., in an effort to improve her outlook. She says that she was encouraged there to think and behave in offbeat ways to free her from her subconscious fears. In one session she was urged to imagine that she was a strand of human hair, because of a job-related project that was troubling her, and she credits that experience with helping her to suggest a new Gillette product called Silkience, a shampoo and hair conditioner.

Ms. Lawrence's experience, like that of many others, suggests that anyone who wants to think creatively should direct his exploration toward *needs*. Old aphorisms are usually reliable because they are based on the distilled wisdom of past experience. One we all remember says, "Necessity is the mother of invention." When we really need something, we invent it. Make a practice of asking yourself, "What will make this product or service of mine more acceptable to my superiors and the public, more fitted to their needs, and better than that of our competition?" Stifle those inner fears and you will start thinking creatively.

There are some who would label the two groups of workers a bit differently from Bob Jenkins's work processors and creative thinkers. They talk about the *doers* and the *dreamers*. That, of course, is only an exercise in semantics. The doers are the men of action and the dreamers are those who think beyond the obvious. Haven't some of your most imaginative ideas come to you when you were completely relaxed, lazily going from one random thought to another with no particular purpose in mind? Only the thinking person who holds to a dream ideal with conviction and determination has a very practical chance of making that dream a reality.

Alexander Hamilton was a standout among that exceptional group of men who formed the shape of our fledgling republic during the final quarter of the eighteenth century. He fought in the Revolution, was an aide to General Washington, helped write the Articles of Confederation, and ardently advocated a strong central government, against bitter opposition. As our first secretary of the Treasury, he planned and initiated the policies establishing our national fiscal system, stimulating trade and enterprise, developing national resources, and placing public credit on a sound basis. Alexander Hamilton was clearly one of the most creative thinkers in the early days of this country.

That makes it all the more interesting to hear, in his own words, just how he went about it: "Men give me credit for some genius. All the genius I have lies in this: When I have a subject in hand, I study it profoundly. Day and night it is before me. My mind is pervaded with it. Then the effort which I have made is what people are pleased to call 'the fruit of genius.' It is the fruit of labor and thought."

Hamilton's modest statement is both encouraging and motivating. It demonstrates that creative thinking *can* be achieved by concentration of thought, married to persistence.

How Do We Think Creatively?

Alex Osborn was the distinguished co-founder of the successful Batten, Barton, Durstine and Osborn Advertising Agency. The importance of creative thinking in advertising inspired Osborn to become a creative man of action who authored four books on the creative imagination. After all his years of study on the subject, he was still mystified by it: "Nobody knows *exactly how* babies are born," he wrote. "No wonder, then, that we are still at sea as to *exactly how* ideas are born. Perhaps neither of these mystic processes will ever be fully comprehended. For this reason, it is unlikely that creative procedure will ever be strictly formulated."

Osborn and others who have both studied and practiced creativity realize that the process is necessarily a stop-and-go, catch-as-catch-can operation, one that can never be exact enough to rate as scientific. It may well be impossible ever to teach the full range of creativity. However, it seems entirely likely that one can improve his capacity for creative thinking by concentration and dedicated effort. What can be honestly said is that effort usually should include some or all of the following steps:

Step 1. Define the problem to be solved in very specific terms. Put it in writing. John Dewey said, "A problem well stated is half solved."

Step 2. Assemble all the pertinent data, all the facts about the problem, all its ramifications.

Step 3. List all the possible solutions that occur to you. Rack your brain. List wild, crazy solutions as well as those that seem logical. Piling up hypotheses will likely increase the odds that you will find a creative, workable solution.

Step 4. Forget all that you have done. Try to blot it out of your mind by going fishing, watching baseball, playing golf or tennis, or even seeing a movie. Let it simmer on the back burner for several days. This is the incubation period that requires no effort by you.

Step 5. And this is the tricky part. With luck, when

least expected, comes the flash of illumination, the revelation, the answer! Novelist Edna Ferber once wrote, "A story must simmer in its own juice for months and sometimes even for years before it's ready to serve."

In an address at M.I.T., Alex Osborn summed it up: "I submit that creativity will never be a science—in fact, much of it will always remain a *mystery*, as much of a mystery as 'what makes the heart tick?' At the same time, I submit that creativity is an art—an applied art, a workable art, a *learnable* art—an art in which *all* of us can make ourselves more and more proficient, if we will."

Give It Top Priority

Most men and women in leadership positions, because of the daily pressure of their jobs, never seem to find the time to think creatively about those jobs: to expand their thoughts about what they are doing and how they might do it more effectively.

Knowing they must find the time if they are to reach their ultimate goals, the *achievers* give it a top priority. They *make* the time and *take* the time to think *creatively*.

THE BOTTOM LINE

1. The consistent creative thinker is the most valuable worker in any company because he has the ability

to pinpoint a potential "fire," and offer a solution, before it erupts. The average executive, the work processor, can only scramble to extinguish it.

2. The commercial value of creative thinking is verified by the number of corporations that invest millions sending their executives to workshops designed to teach them that skill.

3. A host of conscious and unconscious fears, inadequate organization, and a lack of time are the strongest barriers against creative thinking in American business.

4. *Make* distraction-free time that will enable you to organize your thoughts, set them down on paper, examine every possible option, let them incubate, and then present them with confidence and enthusiasm. These are the beginning steps in the mystifying process of becoming a creative thinker.

17

BE A
DECISION MAKER

*Indecision is debilitating; it feeds upon itself; it is,
one might almost say, habit-forming. Not only that,
but it is contagious; it transmits itself to others. . . .
Business is dependent upon action. It cannot go
forward by hesitation. Those in executive positions
must fortify themselves with facts and accept responsibility for decisions based upon them. Often
greater risk is involved in postponement than in
making a wrong decision.*

—HARRY ARTHUR HOPF

Have you heard the story about the Maine potato
farmer and his new hired man? The farmer had hired
the extra help because it was harvest time and he had a
pile of potatoes in his farmyard that was six feet high
and long enough to fill a wagon. He told the new man he
wanted him to divide the potatoes into two piles—the
big ones in one pile and the little ones in another.

The farmer came back at noon to check on his
helper's progress and was surprised to find that he
hadn't moved a single potato in four hours. Shocked by

this incredible show of laziness, the farmer demanded to know why the man had done nothing. "Well," the hired hand grimaced, "I don't mind the work. It's all these dang *decisions* that are holding me back!"

This little anecdote was intended as a reminder that it is impossible to get *anything* accomplished unless we are prepared to make decisions. As homespun philosopher Elbert Hubbard, the sage of East Aurora, New York, once said: "It does not take much strength to do things, but it requires great strength to *decide* what to do." No executive can afford to have it said about him that "The only time he ever takes a stand is on the bathroom scale."

When you aspire to become an achiever, your ability to make decisions becomes all-important. When you reach the top, and in responsible positions along the way, you may have thousands of people working under your jurisdiction. They will be the work processors who will only be as effective as the decisions you make. If you have already experienced success because of your decisions, you have caught a glimpse of an old truth: you make the decision that then allows the decision to *make* you.

Decision is another of those strong English words that can be utterly changed by adding the prefix, *in-*. The result of any decision can be good or bad, depending upon the wisdom of your action. *Indecision,* on the other hand, can rarely be viewed in any positive light. An indecisive leader is neither a creative thinker nor a man of action. He's nothing more than a *handwringer!* In other words, leadership demands that you be a decision maker.

The name Lee Iacocca is one of the most instantly

recognizable in America today. We see him regularly on television and read about his various activities in newspapers and magazines. His autobiography remained on all the best-seller lists for months. In that autobiography, *Iacocca*, the chairman of the board of Chrysler Corporation comments:

> If I had to sum up in one word what makes a good manager, I'd say decisiveness. You can use the fanciest computers to gather numbers, but in the end you have to set a timetable and act. And I don't mean rashly. I'm sometimes described as a flamboyant leader and hipshooter, a fly-by-the-seat-of-pants operator. But if that were true, I could never have been successful in business.

The Dangers of Indecision

Let's take a look now at an actual case history that provides a dynamic demonstration of the way a company can prosper or falter, depending on the character of its leader. In this case, only the names have been changed to protect both the innocent and the guilty. A large corporation, notably successful and profitable, was headed for seven years by a self-confident, knowledgeable chief executive who was both progressive and aggressive. When this man—we'll call him Mr. Strong—retired at sixty-five under the company's policy, he was succeeded by a man who was his complete antithesis.

His successor, Mr. Weak, had performed adequately on a lower echelon, but he actually seemed a little surprised that he had landed in a position of such authority and power. In the top job he immediately became unsure of himself, weak, indecisive—a real play-it-safe type. The organization had grown and prospered under Mr. Strong. It began a rapid downhill slide under Mr. Weak.

As often happens in this fast-changing world, the new chief executive was soon overwhelmed with unexpected problems that were his to solve. He seemed on top of things, in the beginning. When his associates presented a problem and several options for his consideration, he listened carefully to all the pros and cons. He then did what every good leader must do: he took the matter under advisement, ostensibly to give it further study. Unfortunately, it was at that point that Mr. Weak earned his name.

What further study actually took place nobody ever knew. Often days and weeks went by while his worried associates heard nothing from the chief. Secretly, Mr. Weak thought that delaying his decision would make the problem eventually go away or simply solve itself, freeing him from the need to face up to it. Surprisingly, many problems did solve themselves. But the solution always turned out to be the worst possible answer to the predicament. Mr. Weak was unable to learn that *no decision* is in itself a decision. It is a decision, in effect, to surrender the responsibility and trust that you have been given.

Mr. Weak's second method of making a decision on a major crisis was equally irresponsible. He would ask one of his executive assistants to find out exactly how Mr. Strong had reacted in the past when faced with either an identical or similar situation. He would then invariably render the same decision. Mr. Weak's reasoning, from his shortsighted viewpoint, was flaw-less: If things went wrong, how could he be blamed for taking the same course that had worked so well for Mr. Strong?

Decisions made on this basis might seem to be fol-lowing the dictum "if it works, don't fix it." In actual fact, they are usually foreordained to failure. Look at it this way: at the best, decisions of this sort only commit the organization to maintaining the status quo. A deci-sion to play it safe means there can be no exploration of new ideas, new services, new products. Mr. Weak failed to realize that conditions might be quite different from what they were when Mr. Strong occupied the office. Predictably, Mr. Weak's decisions—actually the lack of them—eventually cost him his job.

A decision to follow Mr. Weak's example—do nothing or rely totally on the wisdom of the past—could be the most destructive you would ever make. We live in a society in which technology and information are changing *daily*. What was sound practice yesterday may be all wrong today. Experience is, indeed, the greatest teacher, but the revolutionary changes that are taking place may make yesterday's sound decision totally obso-lete.

A leader, a true achiever, must be bold and coura-geous. His job is to find better answers to problems. He must be eager to lead his organization, ever determined to keep ahead of the pack. There is no better example of a hesitancy to keep abreast of the times than that dem-onstrated by the American automobile industry just a few years ago. To be blunt, automakers were caught napping.

America's number-one industry for the past fifty or more years was automobiles. "Two cars in every garage" was a national motto, and U.S. autos set the standards in the world market. That situation changed with dramatic suddenness and disastrous results.

As do so many market leaders, American car manufacturers became complacent. When American workers demanded higher and higher wages, management acquiesced without much of a struggle, passing on the increased costs to the consumers. The auto workers were soon getting thirty dollars per hour and, because there was no realistic foreign competition, Americans began paying more and more for the family car. They had nowhere else to go.

Farsighted foreign manufacturers saw a golden opportunity to crack the world's most affluent market. With their much-lower costs for labor, Germany, Japan, and a host of other countries started making and exporting cars to the United States. Fuel prices were outrageously higher abroad, so the manufacturers were already expert at making cars that were small and gas-efficient. The easy maintenance and dollar value of these foreign imports enabled them to begin making serious inroads into the American market. The high costs of U.S.-made cars caused many people to take a second look at the less-expensive imports.

Then something happened that apparently nobody had been able to anticipate: OPEC entered the scene and raised the price of gasoline astronomically! In just a few years, the price of OPEC oil soared from $2.00 to $30.00 per barrel. The U.S. auto manufacturers were still building big cars with enormous appetites for gasoline. Almost overnight, Americans began to form long lines at the gas stations, paying close to $1.00 for the same gasoline that formerly cost them 30¢ a gallon. The prices continued to climb, to $1.50 per gallon and more, and those prices still have not tumbled back to the original level, although we now hear little about the "gasoline shortage."

This left the highly paid executives of the automobile industry facing some very hard decisions—the kind of make-or-break choices they had not faced since Henry Ford revolutionized the industry by using an assembly line to produce his stripped-down four-cylinder model. Should they attempt to build low-profit small cars to compete with the foreign companies who were already expert at it? Should they continue to turn out the big gas-guzzlers that most Americans seemed to love? Would the price of gasoline stay up or go down? How was the market going to go? These were just a few of the points motorcar executives had to consider when making plans for the future.

In an unbelievably short time, automobile companies went from huge profits to colossal losses. Thousands of workers were laid off for the first time in automobile history. Thousands more had their contracts canceled, and plants were closed all over the country. It became a major business disaster, with the side effects trickling down to all areas of the economy. The hard decisions faced by the industry leaders a few years ago continue today. The up-one-day and down-the-next estimates on the price and availability of gasoline obviously influence the decision on what car the public will buy. It costs billions of dollars to retool an automobile plant, and the executive who must make the final decision about which way the public will go has an awesome responsibility.

Lee Iacocca has shot to world prominence because he inherited an almost-impossible situation. He dared to make the big decisions and came out a winner. Recently, a mild drop in gasoline prices at the pump coupled with a general business recovery spurred a sharp revival in the demand for cars, despite prices that continue to rise. Profits are soaring once again. But what will happen in the next few years? Does anyone know? Whatever the future holds, one thing is certain. The head of every auto company is going to be faced with momentous decisions. He cannot avoid them, and billions of dollars will ride on what he decides.

Business Week magazine carried a story about the changing of the guard at Ford Motor Company. Donald E. Peterson had been elected as the new chairman, and the article attributed some of the problems facing him to Ford's insistence on clinging to past designs and not reacting to the public's demand for smaller, front-wheel–drive cars. The article concluded with a statement that pinpoints the reason every chief automaker must also be a decision maker: "Maintaining the status quo invites disaster in today's fast-changing auto market."

In reality, markets for almost every product or service industry are changing nearly as rapidly as those for the automobile business. That is why there are so many unlimited opportunities for the dedicated achiever today. Creative thinkers who can be decision makers are at a premium. Those who vacillate or attempt to solve today's problems with last year's solutions are doomed to failure.

It Isn't a New Experience

The quickest way to determine your own potential for making decisions is to evaluate your life and career to this point. Thus far we have discussed only the decision-making problems of the leaders of extremely large organizations. But it's unlikely that you have reached this point without making decisions that were, on their own level, equally agonizing and important. Even a high school student must start weighing the advantages of a paying job against those of a higher education. It is impossible to live without facing decisions.

Father Joe Morin, a Catholic priest, received a letter from a teenager who asked a thoughtful question: "How do I go about deciding what principles and values I should live by?" After commending the young man for having the honesty and courage to ask the question and for his recognition that it's impossible to have "too much help" in making such an important decision, Father Morin made this reply:

> Formerly your behavior was based on rules and regulations set down by others—parents, teachers, civil and church leaders, and (yes) peers. Do this and don't do that! This is in and that is out! Now, after sifting and testing all these influences in the laboratory of your own experience it's time to lay claim to what will be *your* philosophy of life. YOU will decide what principles and values you will live by. Thus you become your "own (inner-directed) person."
>
> Inner-directed mature persons also become re-

sponsible decision-makers. They not only make their own decisions but they take responsibility for the consequences of their actions. They no longer blame others for what happens in their lives (the old "devil-made-me-do-it" syndrome). In becoming your own person, you assume responsibility for your feelings and attitudes; you realize there are very few accidents in life, and that most of what happens is the result not of blind chance but of decisions made either by yourself or others. Of course, there will always be uncontrollables in your life, but what does come under your power, you can't side step.

This process of growth assures that you are becoming a self-motivated, self-determined, inner-directed person—jostled and tossed about by countless life forces but not ruled by them. It's the exciting launching of your life adventure.

This magnificent explanation of our higher purposes in life was contained in one of Father Morin's columns, *Dear Padre*, published by Liguori Publications. As a clergyman, the good father answered the teenager on what was intended to be a spiritual level, primarily. But its commonsense approach to both the dangers and rewards of decision making make it worthwhile reading for the officer of any company.

Decision making, on a personal or business level, is the nature of the game. The higher you are able to climb in the world of business, the more frightening these decisions will become, from the standpoint of dollars and cents. Decision making is an absolute—whether the individual who does it runs a delicatessen in Manhattan, an automobile company in Detroit, or a farm in Nebraska. The way these decisions are made will determine who prospers and who fails.

Sharpening Your Own Skills

There is always something of importance riding on every conscious decision we make. Those decisions that are not major are, as we said earlier, handled automatically by the force of habit. Depending upon the amount of reputation, opportunity, risk, or money involved, decision making can be a frightening endeavor. It is simple fear that influences our abilities to make decisions, and that is the first thing that must be overcome.

Dozens of old chestnuts point the way for us— "Faint heart ne'er won fair lady"; "Nothing ventured, nothing gained"; and on and on ad infinitum. It is even more practical to start with the accurate premise that no one, absolutely no one, can be right *all the time.* H. W. Andrews, as quoted in *Forbes Scrapbook,* took a very pragmatic stand on the issue:

> While an open mind is priceless, it is priceless only when its owner has the courage to make a final decision which closes the mind for action after the process of viewing all sides of the question has been completed. Failure to make a decision after due consideration of all the facts will quickly brand a man as unfit for a position of responsibility. Not all of your decisions will be correct. None of us is perfect. But if you get into the habit of making decisions, experience will develop your judgement to a

point where more and more of your decisions will
be right.

Successful leadership, in any field, demands aggressive confidence. An infantry platoon leader will inspire
no confidence in his men if he orders them up a hill to
engage the enemy while he remains at the bottom,
cowering behind a tree. In the same manner, the style
and substance of a business leader ultimately affects the
productivity of his entire company. He must be able to
look the need for a decision squarely in the eye and
come up with a proper solution *most* of the time. Otherwise, to paraphrase President Harry Truman, "If he
can't stand the heat, he should get out of the kitchen!"

That does not mean, in Lee Iacocca's words, that
he should be a "hip shooter or fly-by-the-seat-of-his-
pants operator." Vital decisions should be reached as
quickly as possible, but only after thoughtful consideration. Chester Bowles, founder of an advertising agency,
former governor of Connecticut, U.S. ambassador to
India and Nepal, and bestselling author, says, "When
you approach a problem, strip yourself of preconceived
opinions and prejudice, assemble and learn the facts of
the situation, make the decision which seems to you to
be the most honest, and then stick to it."

A variety of emotions other than fear almost always
play some part in our decisions. Without thoughtful
consideration beforehand, decisions based on emotion
are potentially the worst we can make. We become like
the wealthy widow who bought worthless oil stock because "The salesman was my favorite nephew." Be very
careful about making any decision to prove a point—
"I'm going to do it because I *want* it to succeed." There

are better ways of demonstrating your enthusiasm and your courage.

What are the best ways to approach a decision that must be made? As quickly and calmly as possible would be the catchall advice. On the other hand, there are specific, time-tested steps that have worked extremely well for others over the years. There's a good chance they will work for you, as well.

1. To make certain you have a solid grasp of the subject, write it all down, listing your own positive and negative viewpoints.

2. Get as much input as possible from others whose opinions you trust. Pay much closer attention to the nay-sayers than the habitual yes-men.

3. Carefully examine all the options, all the advantages and disadvantages in the privacy of your own mind, but don't dilly dally!

4. Make your decision and *do it*—with all the vigor you can muster.

There has been enormous progress in our methods of obtaining vital information. Computers can aid us by providing all the salient facts we need almost instantaneously. But in the final analysis, making a big decision is a highly introspective process. The preceding advice is little more than a rehash of the methods used by a well-known achiever who lived more than two hundred years ago: Benjamin Franklin:

When confronted with two courses of action I jot down on a piece of paper all the arguments in favor of each one—then on the opposite side I write down all the arguments pro and con, cancelling them out, one against the other. I take the course indicated by what remains.

Learning to become a decision maker, like all of the other self-management skills discussed in this book, must begin with your own ability to recognize a problem and think it through. It is another vital character trait that is perfected by constant practice. In time, along with other fine leaders, you will relish the opportunity to make the "really big decision," even while you worry about it.

THE BOTTOM LINE

1. The ability to make thoughtful but prompt decisions is the ultimate duty of any leader in any field.

2. Indecisiveness in any leader is the ultimate weakness. Failure to make a decision, for any reason, is a decision to fail.

3. You can conquer the fear of making major work-related decisions by examining the successful decisions you have already made in your daily life. Practice conscious decision making on every level.

4. Make your important decisions quickly after you have studied every aspect of the question, received maximum input from those on both sides of the issue, and had ample time to reach your own thoughtful conclusion.

18

DELEGATING AUTHORITY: A VITAL ADVANTAGE

No man will ever be a big executive who feels that he must, either openly or under cover, follow up every order he gives to see that it is done—nor will he ever develop a capable assistant.

—JOHN LEE MAHIN

Let's assume you have been with your company for several years, have made steady progress upward, and have been handed a prestigious position with heavy responsibility. You know a good showing here will lead to an even bigger job, but you find yourself bogged down with a work load that makes you suddenly insecure about your potential for ever handling a more demanding situation. It could be that you have fallen victim to a shortcoming that affects many hardworking executives—an inability or an unwillingness to delegate authority.

The editors of *Fortune* magazine conducted a poll in 1984 among the chief executive officers of the Fortune 500 companies, considered the largest industrial concerns in the United States. The aim was simple and worthwhile—to allow these top leaders to name their counterparts whom they considered the best at what they did. When the votes were tallied, Reginald Jones of General Electric took the top honors, followed in order of preference by John Swearingen of Standard Oil of Indiana and Henry Singleton of Teledyne.

Interestingly, all three chief executive officers believed in similar styles of management, especially in the importance of properly delegating authority. Each of them revealed that he considered the delegation of authority an almost indispensable aid in getting his own work accomplished.

Reginald Jones was a strong believer in giving young managers freedom to operate within certain guidelines. He shared much of his authority and responsibility with many people, all the way down the line. John Swearingen is a firm believer in delegating authority all the way out to the geologist in the field. He makes certain that each is in control of (and answerable for) a set amount of money to be spent at the person's own discretion. Henry Singleton has given his associates much responsibility since the day he started Teledyne. Although he was a graduate of M.I.T., he claims he had no choice in the matter because he had no special expertise on the high-tech innovations in which his new firm dealt.

When you consider that these three successful leaders were selected by their *peers* as the most outstanding in the nation, it's possible to reach a valid conclusion.

Each places great importance on the delegation of authority. Therefore, the ability and willingness to delegate rate as critical advantages in the struggle to become a leader and an achiever.

Managing: A Minicourse

As we stated at the beginning, this book is not a treatise on organization or the science of management; neither does it pretend to be. We are concerned here with the leader himself: the individual achiever and the way he became one. Understanding the complexities of an option like delegating authority may seem, at first glance, to be rather elemental and simple. But solving the problem of getting someone to do something for *you* requires a refresher course in organizing an undertaking—of first inspiring people to do their *own* jobs.

Stripped down to the bare-bones fundamentals, here's a case in which the *ize* have it. To manage any job effectively, you must first *organize*, then you must *deputize*, and finally you have to *supervise*. There are elaborations on this shorthand formula, of course, but this is the fundamental equation.

You start by determining all the tasks that must be performed to reach the goals of your organization. Next you carefully select the one—or the one hundred—individuals best qualified to handle each of these duties and empower them with the necessary authority to do their jobs. Finally, you check results at periodic and frequent intervals to make certain that the productivity goals you have set are being reached or surpassed.

The preceding could be called a "one-minute

course in organization," narrowed down to its basics. Obviously, the intelligent delegation of authority is one of your basic duties as a leader. Selecting the proper time to deputize can also be reduced to a single sentence: "Never do anything yourself that someone else can do for you equally well if not better." Of course, delegating is never quite as simple as it sounds. Things happen to us that cause us to forget its advantages.

The Drawbacks of Do It Yourself

George Marston spent the first twenty years of his life in the marketing operations of a giant national company. Let's call it Amalgamated Electric. It had seven factories scattered across the land and sales offices in every major U.S. city. Marston started as a salesman in Minneapolis, handling a big-ticket item from the company line. He did his job so well that he was soon promoted to the position of sales manager in Denver.

Some time after George took over the Denver office, the vice-president in charge of marketing at headquarters recognized that he was facing a serious new problem. A marketing revolution had been building since shortly after the conclusion of World War II when many of the 16 million men and women who had been in the service decided to abandon their hometowns to look for better opportunities elsewhere. They established homes in their new locations, started what would be known as the baby boom, and changed the geographical markets of the United States beyond recognition.

For the first time, many large national distributors

saw the need to establish market research departments in their head offices. With the great shifts of population to the Sunbelt and elsewhere, it was important to pinpoint the location of the demographic changes in order to select new and better markets for their special products and services. At Amalgamated Electric, once the duties and responsibilities of the new market research department were defined, it became crucial to appoint the right man to head it.

The marketing vice-president knew that the candidate had to be a longtime employee of the company, one who knew the firm and all its peculiarities. He had to come from somewhere in marketing, have actual experience in selling and sales management in the field, and be someone who had already exhibited a lively interest in the demographics and population shifts that directly influenced the company's sales.

George Marston's name was one of the seven or eight given to the vice-president by the personnel department as likely candidates for the new post. Marston had all the qualifications and was, on paper, the ideal man for the job. When it was offered to him, he accepted with alacrity and enthusiasm. George was assigned office space in the head office building and went right to work developing the new department. He got off to a great start by selecting eight bright young eager beavers as his assistants. All of these people either had some special training in market research or had otherwise demonstrated a significant interest in or aptitude for the work.

However, the great hopes for the new research department began to fade with alarming speed, in the opinion of the vice-president of marketing. He had set up the department with the idea that it would be able to provide him with the immediate information he needed to decide on the best areas to establish new sales offices. He couldn't lose time deploying salesmen to those geographical areas offering the best sales potential. That information was agonizingly slow in reaching him.

An investigation revealed the cause of the delay: George Marston was a one-man bottleneck. He simply could not, or would not, delegate. The top of his desk was covered with a mountain of files; the desks of his bright assistants were clean and empty. George was determined to give the new job his best effort. He was completely engrossed with colored maps, heavy volumes of statistics, and firsthand reports from the field offices. He was doing his level best to keep on top of everything. In the meantime, the eight bright young people he had chosen to help him were left with little to do except work crossword puzzles, read the morning paper, or write plaintive memos upstairs, requesting transfers to more challenging jobs.

Actually, George was too eager to succeed. He made every problem a major one that he, and he alone, could solve. He was so intent on making the correct decisions that he could not bring himself to delegate any authority—or surrender even a little of his responsibility. In reality, he was an inveterate tinkerer. He simply loved to tinker with problems. He became so fascinated by insignificant details that he lost sight of his real mission.

Despite all of his qualifications and enthusiasm, George had an inability to delegate authority that proved to be a crippling weakness. It was the weakness that eventually cost him his job.

Causes of the Problem

Why are people in management positions, like George, often so reluctant to delegate some of their responsibilities and authority to others? One large and successful organization places much of the blame on what it terms the "single-cause syndrome." All of its executives are warned to avoid single-cause thinking in any situation. This company wants its people to refrain from blaming their failures on or crediting their successes to one cause. Common sense informs us that there are usually a number of reasons for either success or failure. Limiting the reasons is a shortcut that can lead to dangerous planning.

An old aphorism that is deeply ingrained in all of us must also take a large share of the blame—"If you want something done *right,* do it yourself!" That philosophy may work well if it concerns some tiny task you request of your three-year-old child, but it is false reasoning when applied to the upper echelons of business. It can lead to wasted time, energy, and money: "It won't be done the way *I* think it should be done, so I'll end up doing it myself anyway," or "I'll waste more time teaching Joe to do it than I will if I do it myself." Doing it yourself is all right if you enjoy tinkering in your home workshop, but it is not the sensible thinking associated with successful leadership.

Deep-seated insecurity also sometimes plays a major role in an otherwise-able executive's reluctance to delegate authority. It can additionally influence the way you accept and recognize the performance of those who work under you. Every executive who feels overworked

should ask himself whether he is doing adequate delegating, and, if he is not, he should examine these possibilities:

1. Is my assistant really after my job?
2. Am I afraid he will do the work better than I
can?
3. Am I afraid to give him either overt praise or
more authority because of my fear that he will replace
me?

If you must pause for deep reflection before answering
any of these hypothetical questions, you are building an
attitude that is completely self-defeating.

The Other Side of the Coin

Those who exhibit insecurity by their failure to share authority and responsibility with their subordinates may
be, in some cases, protecting their own immediate status
at the expense of an opportunity to move up to a higher
position. They fail to realize that the fastest way to a
promotion is to have a solid understudy in the wings,
ready and able to step into their shoes when the time
comes. Enlightened managements actually rate an executive on his ability to find and develop new talent. They
expect a capable manager to recognize the potential
new stars and recommend them for more responsible
jobs within the organization—even if it means transfer-
ring them out of his personal jurisdiction.

You can profit by examining your own position
right now. Can you name at least one man or woman

among your subordinates who could, with a minimum of coaching, take over your job? If you *can't*, start planning to develop a likely candidate. You will be doing yourself a favor, in more ways than one. A confident attitude will impress the top brass that you put the *company's* welfare first, and that, in itself, will make them more amenable to promoting you. After all, it would not be sound practice to move you to a new spot and leave only a vacuum in your position.

In the final analysis, delegating some of your authority is only going to make your work easier. That is something that even today's brilliant young entrepreneurs have been quick to realize. Bill Gates, for example, became something of a business legend before his twenty-first birthday because of the success of Microsoft, the company he founded with money he earned as a teenager. In less than ten years he fashioned his youthful dreams into a multimillion-dollar company, operating almost as a one-man show.

Bill Gates had the desirable singleness of purpose—"We wanted to be a leader in the goal of putting a computer onto every desk and into every home in America"—but he soon realized that it was *necessary* to learn to be a delegator. "It's hard to have one thousand employees moving in one direction and have them feel good about it," he admits. "So it's important to hire people to bear the burden of finance and planning. If you have a vision of great products and want to have an impact on the marketplace, you need the leverage that comes from professional managers."

He has not regretted his decision to share the burden with others. By his thirtieth birthday, Bill Gates's company reported sales that exceeded $140 million.

There are, no doubt, many reasons why some otherwise capable executives fall short when it comes to the art of delegating authority. None of those reasons can be really valid. An executive's primary duty, to himself and to his company, is to perform in a leadership capacity. He cannot give his best effort to that work if he is swamped with work that others should be doing. If he has insufficient trust in the skill of his subordinates, it behooves him either to train them better or to find new ones. The ability to *delegate* and *supervise* can clear the way for your own advancement.

A statement in the June 1984 issue of *Bits and Pieces* summarizes it this way:

> All great leaders have been people who learned this art of delegating. In fact, good leadership is synonymous with it. People who don't learn it cannot be good managers of other people. They will, first of all, limit the amount of work and responsibility they themselves can handle—thus limiting their own future growth. And they will inhibit the initiative of those under them, limiting the efficiency of the entire group. People who are bent on making the most of their future, their own success, must realize that the art of delegating authority lies at the very heart of leadership.

THE BOTTOM LINE

1. Delegating authority and responsibility and supervising the results are two of the most basic functions of management. Successful leaders use delegating as a practical method of improving their own performance.

2. A fear of being overshadowed by ambitious subordinates is the primary reason many executives fail to delegate. This destructive thinking always backfires because top management gives high ratings to executives who develop important new talent.

3. Confidently select your brightest assistant and give him the necessary authority to take over those responsibilities that he can handle as well as you. His help, and that of others on your staff, will increase your quality time for more important projects and clear the way for your own advancement.

19

BEWARE OF
THE IVORY TOWER

*An executive cannot gradually dismiss details. . . .
It is not possible for an executive to hold himself
aloof from anything.*
—HARVEY S. FIRESTONE

It is the height of irony that an individual who has
played by all the rules—one who has a passionate feeling for his work, has learned his business from the bottom up, has thought creatively and delegated
wisely—faces another problem as soon as he settles into
the new office that symbolizes the achievement of his
goals. It's an insidious disease that plagues all top leaders from presidents of the United States to the officers of
major organizations. It can be called the ivory tower
syndrome or, in blunter language, *executive isolation.*

During the student protests over the Vietnam War in the late 1960s, the president of a major university called in police to maintain order on the campus. The police presence only further inflamed the protesters, resulting in open rioting and widespread destruction of university property. The president's decision was hasty and faulty, based on improper information. As one of his critics commented, "He hasn't talked to anyone under thirty since *he* was thirty!"

Executive isolation becomes more of a factor with every upward move on the leadership ladder. The more he distances himself from the *roots* of the business he loved on the way up, the more difficult it becomes for the rising executive to keep abreast of what is really happening in that business.

The automobile industry (again) offers us a perfect example of the havoc that executive isolation can cause. In January 1982, one of the large automobile companies opened contract negotiations with the United Automobile Workers union. The company announced that it wanted to cut labor costs in order to pass on the savings to new car buyers. That proved to be a calamitous decision that might not have been made if top management had had input from the dealers who were in daily contact with the buying public and *knew* what effect the announcement would have.

As it was, the company and the union continued to disagree, and the stalemate lasted for months. The potential buyers of new cars were, quite logically, determined to wait for the promised reduction in prices while management and labor continued their bargaining. New-car sales almost came to a complete halt before the management won significant concessions from the union, including certain give-backs on wages and fringe benefits. But the comedy of errors was not yet over.

To add fuel to a still-smoldering fire, on the very day that the company signed the union contract, it announced increased bonuses for its top executives. Needless to say, the union workers were furious. And, to make matters still worse, the company did *not* pass along the promised savings to the customers in the form of lower car prices. The new-car dealers were nearly as outraged as their prospective customers, who had reason to feel that they had been misled.

Plummeting sales then forced the company to let go or furlough tens of thousands of blue-collar workers and to institute a freeze on the salaries of white-collar employees. At the peak of these dismissals, in something of a weak apology, top management announced that it was giving itself a salary cut. This later proved to be only a *token* cut! It would be fair to assume that the company's executive leadership had lost some of its touch with reality—not to mention its workers, its dealers, its salesmen, and much of the general public. It was a classic example of the disastrous effects of executive isolation.

The Causes of Executive Isolation

Why is it that so many individuals who reach the top of their fields find themselves isolated, mentally and physically, from the actual work excitement that carried them there? Often, that isolation is something else that comes with the territory. The wave of terror that has engulfed the world almost makes it necessary to build a wall around many leaders. They need real protection from abduction, extortion, and murder. They also need protection, to an even greater extent, from threats to their privacy and the ability to carry on their work.

If an unwelcome visitor to a top leader's organization gets past the security guards, he finds the battlements manned by the individual's first-line troops—the executive assistant who often acts as the alter ego and the executive secretary who may know as much about the business as the boss. This well-meaning convoy and others—close associates, friends, and even the chauffeur—not only protect but *insulate* the top executive from the real world. He seldom has an opportunity to listen to the views of either his employees or the average citizens who make up 90 percent of the country's producers and consumers.

The top people of large concerns also have the ever-present problem of inadequate communication. In organizations made up of thousands of people, it is a long distance from the bottom to the top. It has been proved that even the simplest story is almost unrecognizable after it has gone through the mouths and imaginations of only ten people. The many levels of management between the worker on the floor and the CEO always make the passing of information troublesome. Important details often get shunted aside before they reach the top level, and the chief is then forced to make his decisions on the basis of inadequate and even incorrect information. The built-in isolation of the key posts often makes the occupants unaware of the existence of the problem.

The rising young executive must decide early in the game that he will not become a hapless victim of isolation. He will find that this becomes an increasing danger with each promotion he earns. His whole environment, the circumstances and conditions in which he lives, inevitably undergoes a complete evolution. In the beginning, he will probably have to endure frequent transfers—sometimes as many as five major moves in as little as ten years. Obviously, this can have a disruptive effect on his personal life. It is also the beginning of a long process that can take him ever-further from the world of reality.

When he began his work, whatever it was, he was in almost constant contact with the very people who were, in one way or another, the eventual customers for his product or service. He lived with them and knew them. But, after a series of promotions and transfers, he finds himself at the head office, almost always located in an impersonal big city. He rides to the office in a company car, possibly driven by a chauffeur; has lunch with his closest colleagues in the officers' dining room or a private club; and spends his once-a-week leisure on the golf course or tennis court with the same people. His person-to-person contact becomes homogenized—an endless round of base-touching with individuals who live alike, work alike, and think alike.

That kind of success is heady stuff that can tempt anyone to lose sight of reality, as Jim Wallace discovered. At the age of twenty-nine, Jim opened a small clothing store in a suburb of Chicago. He had little capital—only enough to rent a storefront, stock it, hire one clerk, and open the door. Jim was the purchasing agent, the sales manager, half of the sales force, the bookkeeper and accountant, the treasurer, advertising manager, and part-time janitor. But the business prospered beyond Jim's greatest expectations.

It became necessary to move to bigger quarters over the years until Wallace found himself the owner of a huge and impressive clothing store. Jim now employed a large sales staff, departmentalized, brought in outside specialists, and opted to take on a number two and number three man to help manage the growing concern. Before long, Jim was literally on top of everything—in an executive penthouse suite on the top floor of a skyscraper. He had realized his ambition, but he felt strangely out of sorts.

Since Jim had delegated all his former executive functions to his management team, as prescribed by the best management experts, he found himself talking only to his number two and number three managers and, only occasionally, to a department head. He began to feel like an outsider in the company he had formed. He no longer knew his employees by their first name, hardly even *knew* any of them at all. The customers, many of whom had personally bought their first pair of long pants from Jim, became only faceless, nameless identities who made the cash register ring. The fact that he missed the pace and excitement of the selling floor was the first warning Jim Wallace had that he was no longer in the clothing business—he was only a man expected to make the *big* decisions. With little or no contact with employees and customers, he felt isolated, unhappy, and insecure about his ability to make those decisions.

Don't Be Left Out

This gradual isolation from reality is a very real trap into which any young executive can fall. It can dangerously influence the decisions you make. Delegation, if improperly used, can turn against you. As you go up in any organization, more and more layers of management people come between you, your employees, and your customers. You must fight to keep your lines of real communication open. You must make *certain* that communication comes up to you from the bottom, in accordance with business management theory.

The failure of communication can have a direct effect on the well-known bottom line. Because of that, many organizations now employ a variety of methods to overcome this problem. Here are some of them.

1. *Advisory committees.* Either elected by their peers or chosen by top management, the members are key employees, foremen, leading salesmen, branch or store managers, and dealers, depending upon the problems being discussed.

2. *Job-satisfaction surveys.* A carefully worded questionnaire is sent to all managers, all field representatives, or *all* employees inquiring into all phases of the work that lead to job satisfaction or dissatisfaction. Responses may or may not be signed. Management then has the option of taking appropriate action.

3. *Suggestion boxes.* One of the oldest methods of eliciting anonymous ideas for improvements or general practices that need changing. Many companies now offer valuable prizes for the signed suggestions that are judged most worthwhile.

4. *Customer surveys.* Questionnaires inviting criticisms and suggestions for improved services, usually made available for customers at the point of service. Mailing envelopes are provided. These questionnaires have been used successfully for years by hotels, motels, and restaurants.

5. *Market surveys.* Usually conducted by independent survey organizations who sample the buying public to find out which new products are desirable, the ways present products or services might be improved, and the potential success of a new product or service introduced in selected test markets.

6. *Board representation.* A controversial idea that has not yet been adopted widely. A corporation invites a knowledgeable employee, possibly a field manager, to serve on its board of directors. The intent is to get a lower-level viewpoint on the problems facing the top management.

All these programs emphasize the importance of good information from a wide variety of sources. In too many organizations, the chief executive officer must rely solely on his top subordinates to fill him in on the expected reaction of field management, employees, dealers, and customers to certain proposed courses of action. However, the subordinates sometimes give their boss what they believe he wants to hear rather than honest opinions that might differ from his. At other times some assistants simply have no idea of the way these influential groups will react, but rather than admit their ignorance, they come up with information that is vague, incomplete, and even inaccurate.

It becomes readily apparent that everything depends on the key executive, the style in which he deals with his subordinates, and the actions he takes to keep himself from becoming isolated from the *real world.* Every leader, even before he reaches the pinnacle of success, must not allow himself to become so concerned with his specific area of expertise that he forgets the overall aims of the company that employs him. When he delegates authority, he must inform his subordinates that he wants straight answers and accurate information instead of an ego massage. He must always keep himself informed in every way possible.

Above all, he must continue to *reach out*—to those who work under him, to his clients and customers, and to ordinary members of the community. The ivory tower syndrome can affect leaders at every level. The farmer can familiarize himself with every agricultural theory ever devised, but he'll have trouble raising a good crop until his fingers actually dig into the soil. The individual who refuses to isolate himself will be the one inspired to the most creative thinking and the kind of worthy decisions that will ultimately propel him to the CEO's desk.

Not long ago, the five members of the top management committee of a giant multinational corporation met behind closed doors to work out a well-publicized and thorny problem. One of the members gave an anonymous account of the settlement to a reporter: "The proposal was voted *down,* four yeses to one no. The one dissenting vote came from the CEO."

The good leader is the one who is always prepared to make the final decision, even if it is unpopular. He has been given the responsibility and the authority. He doesn't always get the credit when things go right, but he is the first one blamed when things go wrong. He *must* have a total grasp of the situation before he can make a decision. Executive isolation can make that an impossibility. The sign on Harry Truman's desk said it all:

THE BUCK STOPS HERE.

THE BOTTOM LINE

1. The higher an executive goes in any company, the more susceptible he becomes to the damage of executive isolation.

2. When a leader limits his intimate circle to those who work alike, live alike, and think alike, he is also limiting his access to knowledge about the real world from which he came.

3. Delegate authority, but with the firm understanding that your subordinates are to furnish you information that is accurate and honest. *Reach out* for valid opinions wherever possible.

20

TAKE IT ALL
IN STRIDE

It is said it is far more difficult to hold and main-
tain leadership than it is to attain it. Success is a
ruthless competitor, for it flatters and nourishes our
weaknesses and lulls us into complacency. We bask
in the sunshine of accomplishment and lose the
spirit of humility which helps us visualize all the
factors which have contributed to our success.
—SAMUEL J. TILDEN

When you have finally *arrived*, take time to remember
the object lesson taught us by an anonymous window
washer. You don't know the story? It's a sad but simple
tale: The man had done a particularly good job cleaning
a window on the 113th floor of the Empire State Building and made the mistake of stepping back to admire his
work!

The point is, getting carried away with the excel-
lence of one's own work can be decidedly unhealthy.
Self-congratulation can lead to self-infatuation, and it's

likely that more people have survived failure than have come through success unscathed. The great truth of this statement should be a warning to all of us.

How many times have you heard someone say, "He couldn't stand success"? Or as they often say in the world of sports, "He began to believe his own press notices."

The plaudits of the crowds can easily go to the head; because success is a heady thing. We all need a constant reminder that in life, as well as in sports, "You're a hero today and a bum tomorrow!" Fame is transitory.

When success does come, the successful achiever can be overwhelmed with the excessive praise of his admirers and his head can become too big for his hat. If this happens, he may stop his forward progress and sit back to enjoy his new status as an achiever. And sitting back on one's laurels can be as dangerous as the window washer stepping back to admire his work.

Many people over thirty-five or so have a vivid recollection of a cool autumn afternoon in Yankee Stadium, the setting for a sports story that was both glorious and tragic. It was October 8, 1956, the fifth game of the Sixty-ninth World Series of baseball between the New York Yankees and the Brooklyn Dodgers. The players and managers of the American and National League Champions ran onto the field for their formal introductions, Lucy Munro sang the national anthem as the flag was raised in center field, the mayor of New York City threw out the first ball, and the game was on.

None of the seventy thousand fans who crowded the stands could have anticipated the drama that was about to unfold. They were in for a history-making day.

Six-foot-two Don Larsen, the Yankee starter, was a pitcher that day who went without the customary windup when he fired the ball to the plate. His first pitch was a strike, and the Yankee fans were pleased that their man seemed to have good stuff. Just how good it was became increasingly apparent to the Dodgers as the game progressed. When it was over, not a single Brooklyn batter had managed a hit, or even a walk, off the Yankee starter. Don Larsen had pitched the first and only no-hit, no-walk World Series game in baseball history—the perfect game!

Larsen had already been recognized as a *good* pitcher, good enough to pitch the opener of a World Series, but he became baseball's biggest hero, literally overnight. The winter of 1956/57 saw pages and pages of articles recounting Larsen's remarkable feat. He was fast becoming a legend in his own time, and the Yankee fans could hardly wait for the start of the new season. But something happened to Larsen during the six months from October to May, and he never again approached the form that had electrified the baseball world.

The new season saw him knocked out of the box in many of his early starts, he went on to suffer one loss after another, and the Yankees finally decided to trade the "perfect-gamer" to Kansas City in December 1959. His record was equally poor there, and he was traded to the San Francisco Giants. Later he pitched for several other teams and then drifted out of baseball altogether. His downfall was as precipitous as was his sudden rise to fame. Little has been heard of him since.

There's a saying in the sports world that applies to most other worlds too, "You can't win this year's ball games with last year's scores." As military strategists say, "You may win *one* battle, but the ultimate question is, who will win the war?"

Once you fall into the trap of believing your own press notices, you are headed for trouble. It's the fighter who answers the bell and comes up for the final round who wins the fight. Not necessarily the one who was picked by all the experts to win.

A man who comes from humble beginnings and who experiences great success early in his career is certain to receive many kudos from his admirers and his friends. Suddenly he finds himself the center of attraction. It is heady stuff! He may begin to believe what people write and say about him.

Developing an attitude that enables you to take it all in stride will protect you against the excesses of both *temporary* success and failure. As renowned baseball philosopher Yogi Berra points out, "It ain't over till it's over." That bit of wisdom applies to a ball game, a career, and a life. Our successes can put us into as much emotional agony as our failures, and the trick is to *learn* from both. That was a lesson that Rex Reed, the most widely read motion-picture critic in America, absorbed—the hard way. He nearly chose the wrong career.

"I came out of the womb opinionated," Reed said recently, "all of which made for much controversy in my early days."

His well-intentioned but controversial articles on racial policies at various southern universities, written for the campus newspaper while he was a student at the University of Louisville, earned him the enmity of a majority of his fellow students and the college administrators. Undaunted, Rex headed for New York after graduation, intent on becoming a hard-hitting reporter for one of the big daily newspapers. He quickly discovered that was an ambition not easily fulfilled. Still, he managed to land a job in public relations at 20th Century–Fox's Manhattan office. That success proved to be short-lived, and Reed was one of the first dropped in the film company's economic cutbacks. He spent the next twenty-six weeks on the unemployment lines, wondering what to try next.

He had always been fascinated by movies and acting, and, on money borrowed from his father, he enrolled in classes at the famous Actors Studio. He loved the excitement of acting and was overjoyed when Elia Kazan, one of the world's most noted directors, confirmed his own opinion that he had *talent* and a possibly glorious future in his new career. To back up his opinion, Kazan hired him to play a role in an out-of-town production of Tennessee Williams's great play *The Glass Menagerie.*

Reed was convinced that his decision to try acting was the turning point of his life. The play, and Rex, received ecstatic reviews. Success was his! As he put it, he became drunk on his own perfume. The play had been produced at the Anaconda Mine in Montana, and it closed after a brief but successful run.

Rex returned to the Great White Way with his collection of rave reviews. He was astonished to learn that no one there even knew that he had been out of town.

Rex Reed's great but short ego trip into the world of acting came to a screeching halt. A good thing, too.

The great self-satisfaction he had developed about his acting ability might have lured him into a life of frustration and failure as an actor.

But, combining his great love for writing and his great love for the movies, Reed ultimately found himself writing reviews of motion pictures for newspapers and magazines. A job he loves and does supremely well. He has become an outstanding achiever in spite of his early self-infatuation.

It's pretty much taken for granted that people in high-profile occupations have a difficult time knowing exactly *who* they are after they have been swamped with so much public adulation. But reputations and countless millions of dollars can be squandered as easily in corporate boardrooms as in the political or the sports arena. A rampant ego, overfed by recent success, is no nurturer of practical thinking. At its worst, it becomes megalomania—a delusional mental disorder marked by infantile feelings of personal omnipotence and grandeur.

Adolf Hitler furnishes us with the prime example of megalomania. A "nobody" at the age of forty—former housepainter, paperhanger, and small-time politician— he used strong-arm methods to seize power in Germany after the death of President Hindenburg and became increasingly consumed with egotistic ambition. Calling himself "Der Führer," he had the delusion that he was fated to be the leader of the whole human race—or at least all of it that in his opinion was "fit" to live. Blinded by his own power, carried away by the sound of his own voice, he attempted to make the delusion a reality by plunging the whole world into a war that destroyed millions of lives. Of course, his madness also destroyed him and his Reich that was supposed to endure for a thousand years.

Fortunately, there are few cases of megalomania coupled with the kind of power Hitler was able to use. But it is possible to sense something that might be called *creeping* megalomania in some of our leaders in every field. When the ego gets out of hand, when any leader is unable to take his success in stride, he is in danger of becoming a victim of incipient megalomania, which can make him his own worst enemy. It need not happen! The real test of anyone who gets "too much too soon" is the manner in which he or she handles it.

Actress Sally Field is an excellent example of someone who has taken enormous success in stride. She starred in three hit television shows before the age of twenty-five; she won an Emmy for the TV movie *Sybil* in 1976 at the age of thirty; she won two Oscars for best actress while she was still in her thirties, an achievement that had never before been equaled. She was seen frequently at nightclubs with many of the leading male stars of Hollywood.

With all this success coming to her so early in her career Sally could easily have turned into a supreme egotist carried away with her successes.

In the October 1985 issue of *Harper's Bazaar* Sally Field was featured as one of the most outstanding of the new achievers among women in America.

Sally never felt pressured by her early success. She is quoted as saying,

> I never felt trapped. Eventually I grew on. I grew out of several things. We're all in the process of

shedding skins. And although a lot happened to me at an early age, it never seemed to be back-to-back-to-back. I'm not a person who works constantly. I'm not a workaholic. Even in the old days, I would always go home between projects. Except when I was doing a TV series, which is why I'm not doing them any more, there is a life in between. Now I only make one movie a year or a year and a half.

Sally's new movie, *Murphy's Romance*, in which she stars with James Garner in a contemporary romance, was released last year. This was the first made by her own production company. She not only acted but was her own executive producer.

Over the years Sally has refused to be typed. She has amazed her director and her fans with the variety of parts she has played. In her early days Sally was the ingenue type in "Gidget" and "The Flying Nun" and later the sexy type in such films as *Smokey and the Bandit*. Each time it was difficult to avoid being labeled. But she has been wise in choosing her roles.

"There is so much to do," she says, "so much I have not done. I still don't feel I have even started. Maybe I'll always feel like that, that I've barely touched on doing things, on stretching myself, reaching out. I realize I'm only limited by my own foibles. I have a lot waiting for me out there—if I don't trip up."

This is the story of a young woman who will *never* sit back to admire her work, never rest on her laurels. She will never suffer from creeping megalomania. She is still looking for new worlds to conquer.

There's a little incipient megalomania in the best of us. We all tend to become increasingly proud of our successes. But well-balanced individuals never let their pride get out of control.

So, when you think you have the whole world in the palm of your hand, when you have won every contest you have ever entered, when you begin to think there's no one quite like you, think not of the great things you have done but rather think only of all the things in this world that still need to be done. Then get started.

THE BOTTOM LINE

1. Being able to stand success is something every potential achiever should contemplate long before he arrives at his destination.

2. Overblown recognition for a particular success can nip true achievement in the bud. It is dangerous to rest on your laurels if you want to go one step higher.

3. Remember success can be fleeting, nurture it.

4. The ability to take success in stride is as important as your capacity for rising above failure.

5. Think of all the things in this world that need to be done; make every day count. Today is God's gift to you; what you do with it is your gift to Him.

AFTERWORD

THE TRUE
ACHIEVER

In 400 B.C., the ancient Greeks were not altogether unfamiliar with the art of self-management. Socrates, the
great teacher and philosopher, once said to his pupils in
Athens, "Let him who would move the world first move
himself." That wisdom has lost none of its import over
the centuries, as we have attempted to reiterate in the
pages of this book.

Ambition is another of those English words that can
take on an unpleasant connotation sometimes. And yet,
every successful achiever must have ambition. It is an

admirable trait, so long as the individual is ambitious for worthwhile goals. To have power, a steam engine must have fire under its boiler. Ambition is the fire that drives human beings to achievement.

We have pointed out in this book that every human being can be considered a bundle of habits—unconscious habits that enable us to perform the little daily chores that require no thought, good habits we develop to perfect our characters and our ability to produce, and bad habits that creep into the pathway and impede our progress. There are others we have not discussed because it would be impossible to pinpoint *all* of the virtues and vices that human flesh is heir to.

Each chapter in this book has been designed to highlight one particular habit, personality trait, or working technique that will most seriously affect your personal pursuit of success. Most of these are positive advantages to be perfected; the final two are dangers to be avoided. It is my firm belief that any individual who masters all of these techniques will substantially improve his chances of becoming the achiever he wants to be. And yet, my hat size has not yet increased to the extent that to my mind this is the *only* way a person can achieve his or her goals in life.

Anyone with sufficient self-discipline can be lacking in some of the techniques fostered here and still emerge a winner. In any event, the principal aim of this self-management program is to expose and expand the specific areas in which a thinking individual can discipline himself to use the tools that will help him reach attainable goals. If one cannot manage himself, he will surely fail.

This equation is truthful and all-encompassing.

Consider the man who works for himself. He has no one *but* himself to supervise his activities and inspire or goad him into greater achievement. Any person who moves into a leadership position must be in full control of *himself* if he is to set a good example for those who work under his direction. Intelligence, education, and drive are prime requisites for achievement, but they become virtually worthless if you lack the discipline that will enable you to transport your abilities to the marketplace. That's comparable to paying scalpers' prices for tickets to the Super Bowl and forgetting the location of the stadium.

There is no denying the fact that our main thrust in this book has been toward the achievement of goals that might be considered largely material. That was our deliberate aim, inspired by the exceptional opportunities available today and the obvious need to open them up to skilled, thoughtful, caring people. Wise leadership making proper use of modern technological advances for the benefit of all is the private sector's greatest contribution to our society.

As we said at the beginning, the techniques we have emphasized in this book are synergistic. They relate to and feed on each other. The man or woman who makes a studied effort to master them and use them in daily life will find more joy and satisfaction in his or her work and will become a better *person* in the process. The achievers you have met in this book came from different backgrounds and worked in a wide variety of fields. Each was an authentic *achiever,* in the finest meaning of the word. All of them were bright, dynamic people who reached out, who gave their all in order to realize their dreams.

There is neither a single nor an easy way to true achievement. It is equally impossible to place a dollars-and-cents value on any individual's true worth. We must remember to *put it all together*—all the talents and strengths we have to offer—and give it our best effort, because "getting there" is far more than half the fun.

In the final analysis, a true achiever is any man or woman who has reached his or her full potential as a human being.

INDEX